THE ENTHEOLOGICAL PARADIGM

Essays on the DMT and 5-MeO-DMT Experience

And the Meaning of it All

MARTIN W. BALL, PH.D.

The Entheological Paradigm:
Essays on the DMT and 5-MeO-DMT Experience and the Meaning of it All

Martin W. Ball, Ph.D.

©2011
Kyandara Publishing
All text and art by Martin W. Ball

ISBN: 978-0-578-08080-2

Table of Contents:

Introduction

This book is somewhat different from my previous books on entheogens in that it is a collection of independent essays. In other words, I didn't sit down and start writing and work my way from beginning to end, which is how I usually go about creating a book. Here, these essays and writings were all written at different times and for different purposes. All of them, however, focus on the Entheological Paradigm, the name I've given to the system of understanding I've developed out of my own awakening/transformation.

Entheological can be understood to mean "the logic of God within," and as a paradigm, it is a description of the nature of reality and the nature of being. It is naturalistic in that it avoids any mystification, metaphysics, or what might otherwise be deemed "supernaturalism." While "God" is often thought of as a supernatural force (and therefore dismissed by scientific thinking), here, God is understood as the unified nature of reality and acknowledges that consciousness/life is not a product of material reality but is in fact the organizing principle of reality. In many ways, the Entheological paradigm embraces empirical science while also recognizing the fundamental nature of the mystical experience as the ground for human identity, coupled with an understanding of the human mind, ego, and awareness as an expression of energy. Most spiritual and religious views are rejected by the Entheological Paradigm. The essays that follow articulate the specifics of the Entheological Paradigm and illustrate how it can be applied to actual experience, both analytically and practically.

Given the common theme in all these writings, there is a great deal of overlap and repetition from one essay to the next. However, I have set up the readings to have the most natural and productive flow from one to the next. Thus, the book can either be read straight through, or simply one essay at a time and in no particular order.

The essays, "Terence on DMT," "Energy, Ego, and Entheogens," and "The *Avatar* Dreamhunt" were all originally published at RealitySandwich.com "The Process" was first given as an episode of the *Entheogenic Evolution* Podcast, and is also available in my art book, *Tryptamine Visions/The Process*. The first essay is the transcript of my recent talk at the Science and NonDuality Conference of 2010, which sets up the framework for the essays that follow. "Visionary Art" is the first attempt at a contribution to a book on that subject. "God's Prescription Form" and "My Birthday Wish" were postings to my account on Facebook. "The Entheological Paradigm: An Overview" is the text to a website I created of the same name. "Digesting *The Spirit Molecule*" was originally made available on-line.

Taken together or independently, these writings flesh out the Entheological Paradigm and show how it can be applied to art, film, entheogenic experience, and life and existence in general. It is a theory of everything, after all, and these essays help demonstrate that.

I've written brief introductions for some of the chapters that were not included in the original writing. Otherwise, the essays remain unchanged from their original form.

My intention with sharing all of these writings is to help bring clarity. Having found clarity within myself, I desire to share it with others. Clarity is the one thing that can truly transform this world and the human experience, and that is what I hope to help cultivate in others. Having found my center and uncovered the truth of my being, I want to share this with others. In the grandest sense, I hope to help move humanity from illusion to authentic knowledge of the self and our genuine nature, freed from speculation, projection, attachment, and fantasy.

This is no small thing. Humans have been wondering what it's all about for millennia. Caught in the web of illusion produced by the ego, humans have been telling themselves stories and creating spiritual fantasies for as long as humans have been around. These illusions have helped to nourish and inspire individuals and cultures, but they also provide fertile ground for fear, violence, and self-delusion. Virtually all the problems currently faced by human beings are the products of confused egos: religious violence, political polarization, unbalanced competition, clashes of identity, and much more. What it boils down to is people are busy being what they think they should be and are not being what they truly are. Genuine self-knowledge holds the power for the radical transformation of human society. Indeed, it is the only path to actual liberation and is necessary for our continued evolution, and perhaps survival.

Now is the time for clarity, truth, and authentic being. The challenges that we encounter here on Planet Earth and our complex human societies need clarity, and nothing less. Confusion, illusion, and projection can never solve problems: they only create more. If we truly want to transform, then we need to live in reality.

Clarity comes one person at a time. It is not the result of a belief system or even a philosophy. It is an inner state of truly knowing who and what the self is. From the center, all things are clear. It is a process of encountering our illusions and projections, taking responsibility for them, and moving on. It is a process of awakening to the true nature of the self and a learning of what it truly means to "be yourself." It is a process of letting go, accepting, and allowing. It is a process of finding one's center and then resting securely and confidently in that energetic nexus that is the genuine nature of being.

Many are currently seeking to flesh out a "new paradigm." Often, such attempts combine pseudo-science with spiritualized worldviews. This is particularly true among the New Age and psychedelic communities, where individuals have embraced shamanic, indigenous, and spiritual traditions that incorporate beliefs in spirits, other realms, past lives, and non-physical realities. It is often taken as a sign of spiritual openness to accept the reality of spirits and disembodied intelligences and such is touted as a path to tolerance, acceptance, peace and transformation. As articulated within the Entheological Paradigm, such tendencies are in fact an embracing of illusion and projection.

The Entheological Paradigm thus undertakes the process of separating the wheat from the chaff, so to speak, and addresses the deepest question of: what is really going on here? As such, it is a map to understanding reality as a whole as well as individual experience. It makes sense of the most bizarre and unexpected spiritual and psychedelic experiences without introducing any speculative theories, entities, or concepts. Furthermore, the fundamental truth of this paradigm can be directly experienced by anyone who is willing to undergo the rigors of self-analysis and energetic exploration with the use of entheogens. In the end, it is a framework for being honest with oneself and with others. It is a guide for overcoming our egoic tendencies to project and become attached to our ideas and beliefs. It is a guide for overcoming confusion and illusion with clarity.

For those who read these pages, I wish you the best for your journey, and encourage you to embrace the truth that only by finding the love and clarity within can you truly extend that to others so that we can collectively make this world what we know it can be. It is my hope that these essays will help others toward that end, so that we all may do our individual part to move humanity to the next stage of conscious evolution. In finding the center, may we all find ourselves and find each other in truth.

Martin W. Ball
Feb, 2011

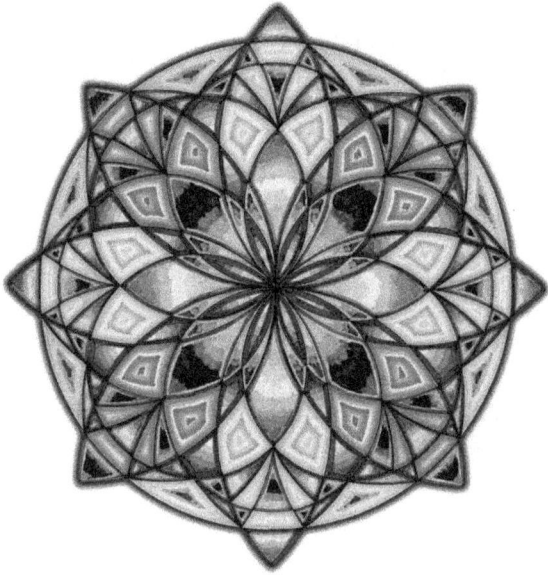

5-MeO-DMT and the Entheological Paradigm

Talk given at the Science and NonDualtiy Conference
San Rafael, California, October, 2010

Introduction:

This is the edited transcript of my presentation at the *Science and NonDuality Conference* in 2010. I've chosen to begin this book with this talk as it introduces most of the ideas that will be explored in greater detail throughout the essays that follow. I've edited the talk for readability, occasionally changing wording, but have not added anything that was not in the original. I make occasional reference to James Oroc, who started off the session discussing his own mystical experiences with 5-MeO-DMT. Significantly, when Oroc and I spoke on this topic, 5-MeO-DMT was still legal. It became listed as an illegal Schedule I substance as of January 19th, 2011.

The session we were speaking in was titled "Entheogens as a Portal," and was concerned with the issue of how entheogens relate to the questions of non-duality and unitary, mystical experiences. My goal in this brief talk was to relate my own process of awakening and getting to know my true nature, what I learned from the process, and how entheogens such as 5-MeO-DMT produce the opportunity for mystical experience and what that tells us about the nature of reality and the nature of the self. For anyone who is interested, a more complete account of my (as then still-incomplete) process of awakening is published as the concluding chapter of my book, *The Entheogenic Evolution: Psychedelics, Consciousness and Awakening the Human Spirit,* and a more detailed account of my first full 5-MeO-DMT experience is published in the introduction of the same book.

The Talk:

My name is Martin Ball, and I'm the author of the book *Being Human: An Entheological Guide to God, Evolution, and the Fractal Energetic Nature of Reality*. Kind of like Roc (James Oroc, author of *Tryptamine Palace*), this book, for me, came out of my experiences with 5-MeO-DMT. Much like Roc, prior to my encounter with 5-MeO-DMT, I would have considered myself, originally, as something of an atheist. I have my Ph.D. in Religious Studies, so I've done a lot of studying of different mystical traditions, comparative mysticism, philosophy of science and religion, and all of this, and really considered myself to be, philosophically, a Buddhist. And if you know anything about Buddhist tradition, then you know that mostly Buddhists will say, "Hey, we're atheists – we don't believe in any kind of creator God." So, I had sort of these Buddhist ideas. I wasn't really a practicing Buddhist, but I did practice meditation and things like that.

But anyway, my very first experience with 5-MeO-DMT - Now, this is very important, because any medicine, any entheogen that you're taking, is always going to open up a reflection of yourself. That's primarily what they are doing. This is important, because, when we say, "Look, you can take an entheogen and you can have an experience of God," remember; that's a reflection of *you*. We're talking about non-duality. We're talking about the unitary nature of reality. There's only *one* actual reality, and that is *you*. Now, it's not the "you" that you *think you are*. It's not the "you" that you've habituated yourself to. It's not the "you" that you've created as a social being in any way. But it absolutely is *you*. Whatever occurs within these experiences is a reflection of you in some way.

So, as an individual, I had always been very much motivated by the quest for *Truth*, by the quest for *Reality*, which is why I went into philosophy, it's why I went into Religious Studies, it's why I studied physics, it's why I looked at all these things. Because I wanted to know: what's really out there? What *is* this reality that we live in? I had that deep motivation within myself. And I credit that with allowing me to have this unitary experience that suddenly occurred.

I was invited by a friend to come over and try 5-MeO-DMT. He said, "Hey, this is a nuclear rocket straight into the heart of God," and he was kind of quoting Oroc. So I said, "Well, OK . . .We'll see. I don't believe in God, but you know, go for it, bring it on!"

We were using this vaporizer and it had this little piston. And so you fill up this chamber with vapor – it was probably about 15-20 mg of 5-

MeO-DMT, which is not very much – we're talking very small amounts of this little crystalline compound. And you know, I have this little thing and I see the piston go down as I'm taking in the hit, and then . . . *Oh my God!*

Everything dissolved into this pure fractal mandala of just crystal-pure white light, and I just went . . . And the first thing out of my mouth was just, "Thank you God!" And for the next hour, that's all I did – I'm just lying there, saying, "Thank you! Thank you!"

I was just absolutely overwhelmed. I mean, "Oh my God! Oh my God! This is God! This *actually is God! This is True! This is Reality!*"

And that startled the hell out of me. Because then I came back from that experience and I was like, "Wow . . . what just happened? How is this possible? That is the most amazing thing that has ever happened to me, hands down." And from that moment on, I said, "Oh yeah – God is real."

But this was very interesting for me, because I had always kind of struggled with this issue of belief. I had studied all these religions and all these beliefs and I was never interested in belief, never interested in faith. At this point I can say, absolutely, "Yeah, God's real. No, I don't *believe* in God. There's no need to *believe* in something that's real. That's like asking, 'Do you believe in your hand?' Um – you know, my hand's right here. I don't need to believe in it because it's right here. It's something that's present within my reality. It is something that is *undeniable* within my reality." And that's what this experience did to me. "Wow – this is real. This is absolutely real."

So, I kept going back to this experience because this was absolutely amazing. It just blew everything out of everything that I ever thought about everything – It was all shifting and changing. And, in agreement with Roc, what's occurring here is that this is absolutely the most powerful tool we have to help get your ego out of the way. I've had a lot of experience with this now, and I've also had a lot of experience in working with this medicine with other people, and I now know, absolutely, that it is 100% an individual choice. It is always a reflection of that individual who is taking the medicine, because people whose egos don't want to let go, you can give them so much medicine . . . the amounts of medicine that for me, I'm thinking, "My God, I can't believe this person is still holding on!" But, people can.

So, it's not a "magic bullet" in any sense. It is very, very magical in the sense that it provides an opportunity to have these massively expansive experiences and enter into unitary states of consciousness, but if you want to resist it, if your ego decides, "I cannot handle this. This is too much," you will be able to resist it. You will be absolutely miserable and terrified. It will be horrific. It might actually cause you to lose your sanity for some period of time. But every individual has the capacity to hold onto their crap as much as they want.

Fortunately for me, for this body and for this perspective, I was able to let go of all that stuff very, very quickly. This also coincides with the fact that it came just after I had gotten divorced, just left my job – I had decided that I had been living a life where I had basically been using my ego to keep myself clamped down and I was being things that other people wanted me to be, and I wasn't actually being myself. So I had just made all these radical changes in my life and said, "Look – I'm going to figure out who I am. I want to know what's really important to *me*, not what's important to everybody else in my life. And I want to be authentic and true to that."

So I was in the right space for me to encounter that complete unitary experience. Not everybody is. And a lot of people who think they are, they come over and they work with me with the medicine, and they're clearly not ready. I've worked with plenty of people who have spent their entire lives meditating – I've worked with yogis and mystics, I've worked with Tibetan Buddhists, Sufi mystics, Kabbalists, ministers have come over – I've had people all across the spectrum come over, and most people simply aren't there. They're not ready. Even if they think they are. Even if they think, "Hey, I've been meditating my whole life."

And honestly, I've found the people who've meditated a whole lot have a lot more to hold onto than many people do, actually, because they've created all of these high-level egoic structures where they reorganize their ego so that they can get into very expansive states, but they're not able to go all the way. What happens when they're confronted with that infinite energy? They hold on with their breath. They're very poised. They're there, because they've learned how to do this in meditation, but they're not letting go. They're not going all the way.

It's a process of helping people learn how to get beyond their meditation practice, get beyond their breathing practice, get beyond all of those things. And that's what it takes for most people, because the truth is you have no idea what your infinite nature is actually like. Whatever idea you have of it, that's not it! That's a guarantee. If you have an idea of what you think it is, then that's not it. And if you've had an experience where you think, "Oh, I can definitely identify that," that's not it. Because that's an *it*. We're talking about non-duality. We're not talking about specific, discrete states of consciousness or discrete experiences. We're talking about the *totality of everything*.

Anyway, to get back into my own personal story, the next thing that started to occur with me after going back and then revisiting this medicine – as my ego is completely gone – and, in agreement with Roc, in those states, there's really no concept of my body, no concept of this idea of "Martin," no concept of the idea of who I am or where I came from or anything like that - there was a profound sense within that of "I AM!"

What is that "I"?   I don't know, but damn, I *certainly AM*. There is no denying that!

So my ego would get out of the way, and then the most bizarre thing would happen – at least, from my perspective, as I'm able to witness this from inside myself. What would happen is I would start speaking. And actually my body would get very symmetrical. My hands would tend to go out, and then I'd start saying things. But it wasn't *Martin's* voice. As a matter of fact, it was very different. My voice would get much deeper, much more resonant, and it would say, "I am Everything. I am all that there has ever been. I am all that there ever shall be. I am energy and I am infinite. I am the life inside of your heart for I am you!" And then the medicine would wear off and I'd look around the room and say, "Uh . . . did you people just hear that?" "Yeah . . ." "Who's talking?"

This was a real conundrum for me because this was not Martin's voice – Martin had no idea what was going to be said, and every time I took 5-MeO, it would be stuff like that, but it would always be different and I could never predict what was going to come out. So from that point on, I just called it "The Voice."

And then I found, having been introduced to these unitary states of consciousness through 5-MeO-DMT, that this was happening to me actually all the time, not just when I was taking the medicine. And also, at that point, when I took any other psychedelic, any lower-order psychedelic, I found that I could get into conversations with the Voice. And it was fascinating because Martin would ask a question, in the Martin voice, and then the answer would come back in this very authoritative voice. And this was very, very confusing for me for quite some time because I actually felt rather schizophrenic.   There's this "Martin" identity and there's this universal, pure energy identity that keeps coming out of me.

I took 5-MeO-DMT one time and the Voice says, "I will do it in this body!" I came back from that and asked, "What the hell is happening to me? This is bizarre. I don't know what's going on." So, I was a little sacred. I was a little sacred that there's something going on here and I clearly don't have any control over it, but it's this unitary consciousness that keeps coming through.

And honestly, I reached a point where there stopped being any distinction at all. And what I've found is that it's just a reflection of my energy. So here now, as I'm talking with all of you, I sound a little bit more like "Martin." But actually my voice has changed. My voice is not the same as it was before all this started. So, here I sound a little more like "Martin" because here we're operating in a dualistic fashion. I'm here, you're there, I'm the one speaking to you, producing the words, and you're the ones who are listening, so we're in more of a "regular," dualistic consciousness. Depending on the topic of conversation, though, I can very quickly slip down into "the Voice." And what happens, actually, is that my body becomes symmetrical when that occurs, so it's difficult for me to do it with the microphone in my hand because I can't be symmetrical. I have to be asymmetrical.

So I went through this whole process of trying to come to grips with who and what I was. Now, I'm very comfortable saying this. I'm not ashamed to say this and I'll also insist that no, I'm not insane. I'm actually perfectly rational. But from a non-dual perspective I'm perfectly happy to say, "Sure – I'm God." That's exactly what I am. I know that. It's not a belief. It's not an issue of faith. It's not an idea. It's simply reality, and I know it. And I've reached the point where my ego does not have that death grip on me anymore so that I'm able to move through my energy very freely and I can express it. And that was a very radical process for me to go through.

But also understand that that's a completely non-egoic statement because guess what? You're God too! So, it's not *just* me. It's not like I'm saying, "Hey, I'm God, so everybody, you know, bow down." No. There's only *One*. That's the clear conclusion that I reached through all of this – that there's actually only *One Being*, and that one being likes to produce itself in multiple forms, and here we are. "Hello! Hello self! It's great to see you."

What really occurred within me was this massive energetic shift within my body, within my being. And by working with that energy, and understanding that in myself – you see, if I can understand myself, I can understand everything because I'm God - so I had to learn to understand this in myself, and then help other people with understanding this as well. Now what I've come up with is what I call *The Entheological Paradigm*, and my book, *Being Human,* is basically the book I wrote about this. It's a really short book. It's about 109 pages and it has a complete description of the unitary nature of reality and how you can figure it out for yourself.

It's actually quite simple. What it does come down to is that we live in an extraordinarily complex and sophisticated energetic system, which is *us*, which is what *we are*, which is what *I am*, which is what *you are*, and it works on relatively simple principles, which I'll return to in a moment.

As an aside, working in the psychedelic/entheogenic community, most of them are not actually interested in non-dual states of consciousness. In my sharing this, I piss a lot of people off. I piss a huge number of people off because a lot people want to talk about how they want to take DMT and they want to talk to machine elves and angels and ascend to other realms and they want to have all these dualistic experiences. And I've come back and said, "Those are all reflections of yourself. They're all reflections of your ego." This really makes people angry because their egos are very attached to these ideas and they want to talk to machine elves, they want to have these experiences. But most of these are people who are working with DMT, and as Roc has pointed out, 5-MeO-DMT takes you well beyond what's going on with the DMT experience, for the most part. Thus, actually producing a model for the unitary nature of reality and how it relates to entheogens is not very well received within the psychedelic community because there's a lot of attachment to dualism there. But anyway, this is the information that I've been putting out, so I like to talk about: what is the nature of reality? What is going on?

The conclusion that I've come to, and all of my experiences bear this out as true, at this point, is, "Look, this is the nature of reality." Sometimes people get mad at me for saying that because they say, "Well, how do you know?" Well, it just is . . .

Reality is a fractal energetic system. What is God? God is a fractal energetic being. All things that exist are energy. Your thoughts are energy. Your emotions are energy. Your body is energy. Everything in this room is energy. Everything that's not in this room is energy. *Everything is a form of energy.* Many different spectrums, many different kinds of energies, but everything is energy.

And if we look around reality, we can see that pretty much everything is a fractal. Everything has certain geometric proportions and ratios and mathematical properties. Fractal mathematics were basically developed back in the 1970s, and what mathematicians have found now is that really everything in nature appears to exhibit fractal properties. Clouds, rivers, mountains, your DNA, your heartbeat, your vascular system, your nervous system, the biological structures of living beings, plants, animals, rocks, trees, everything. Everything that exists is a fractal energetic structure. And we can look at "inorganic" reality and we can look at "organic" reality and we see fractal structures. They're everywhere.

So there's a continuity, absolute continuity, between what we identify as organic and what we identify as inorganic. The only division seems to be between mobile beings that self-organize in consciousness and non-mobile energetic structures that don't have self-motivated direction. What we see in living beings like us - animals, plants, things like that - is that we have certain energetic structures that allow for high-level self-conscious processing, especially among human beings. Human beings have egos. There doesn't seem to be any evidence that other animals on this planet actually have egos of the same high-level of self-awareness that we have as human beings. I've never seen a cat ponder an existential question. That's my guess, but there doesn't seem to be a lot of evidence.

Human beings seem to have certain structures within our bodies that allow us to have very high-level self-reflective experiences, and therefore we also have egos. Egos are ultimately collections of energetic constructs that are creating your false sense of self. If we look at reality as the energetic interplay of the One Being, what we clearly have is a being that's playing with itself. It's actually playing games with itself in the sense that there is the supposed self and the conventional other that exists outside of this supposed self. And that's really the only way to play a game. If there's only one being, you've really got to make yourself in somewhat deluded form so that you can actually play together. Anyone ever try and play a game of chess by yourself? You can't do it, right? So, what's the One Being doing? It's evolving itself into multiple forms so that it can actually interact with itself and have fun in the reality that actually is itself. But if we were all perfectly conscious of that all the time, we'd all just be in oneness and no one would ever do anything. There wouldn't actually be anything going on within this game we call reality. So, your ego actually is helping you play the game in the sense that it's convincing you that, "Hey, you're a separate being. You've got your own life. You've got all your own responsibilities and you've got your self, so you've got to take care of that self."

As we're maturing, as we're children and we're growing up, we're actually accumulating collections of energetic patterns that we're using to define ourselves, and those are ways that we think about ourselves, the beliefs that we have, the reactions that we cultivate within ourselves, and the behaviors that we then exhibit when we're interacting with others and dealing with the world. Now, all of these are energetic constructs. Everybody has ways that they think, ways that they behave, ways that they believe. The problem is your ego is constantly lying to you because your ego is trying to convince you that you are a particular self when you are not – you're just a representation of the One. The ego, by necessity, is going to create collections of lies, fantasies, and illusions to convince you of certain realities about yourself. And the truth is that they are simply not true. They're just ideas that you have. They're patterns. They're habits. They're energetic constructs.

So, we'll come back to the punch-line of 5-MeO-DMT. What happens? The way that I like to talk about entheogens is to say that they are energetic openers in the sense that they allow you to perceive and experience energy in a heightened fashion. Now, going back to the idea that energy is really the only thing that exists, and that you actually just are energy, these clearly are the most profound tools that we could ever use in order to enter into these energetic states of consciousness because that's simply what they do.

With 5-MeO-DMT you can go from zero to infinity in about 10 seconds, in terms of your energetic experience. In order for that to happen, you must drop your egoic concepts because your egoic concepts are energetic structures that are limiting your energetic experience of the infinite. *You cannot experience the infinite and your ego at the same time.* It's impossible because your ego is a constriction of your energy.

So what happens? You take the medicine and all of a sudden you have this massive experience of expansion into the infinite. If your ego is wise and trusting, your ego will say, "I'll just let go . . . OK, I'll die. I'll get out of the way," and then you can go fully into that unitary experience. But honestly, most people don't do that. Most people use their ego to then try and clamp down on this massive expansion that is happening to them energetically. They try and hold on with their egos in many, many ways.

The last thing that I guess I would share with you that I've found is that when this occurs – and it's with these powerful medicines where you can observe this occurring, because of this massive energetic flood – anyone who manages to get out of their ego becomes symmetrical in their body and they expand. And if people are actually able to move with that energy, their movements become fluid and symmetrical. Therefore, non-egoic, genuine energy in your body is perfectly symmetrical, fluid, and in constant motion. When people release all the way, that's what they do. Anyone who is holding on with their ego will exhibit asymmetrical movement in their body. It's a crystal clear indication – you're in your ego, you're out of your ego. So, someone takes a hit of 5-MeO-DMT and they start to get terrified. What do they do? They turn and they look to the person sitting next to them, "Help me!" Look at that! They just broke their symmetry. Or, they curl up into a fetal position and they're breaking their symmetry. Or the energy is so big and they can't handle it and they're rolling from side to side, madly screaming.

Every single person who releases all the way opens up and becomes symmetrical. Look what's happening in the body. Your arms and legs open because you are opening and expanding. The energy of your consciousness is *always* demonstrated by your body – always and forever. And also, this is now a critique that I have of many of the meditative traditions that say that they promote non-dual consciousness. They're all sitting there with their legs crossed. They're all sitting there with funny positions for their hands. They're not symmetrical in their bodies, and I will tell you, having worked with plenty of people, if they're going all the way, their body is going to open. There is no such thing as having crossed legs and being in complete unitary consciousness. I've never seen it. It just doesn't happen. Just something to think about!

∞	Prescription Form, God's Pharmacy Serving Reality Eternally	∞

Patient: *Confused Humans Everywhere*

Condition: *Inflamed Ego*

Medicine: *5-MeO-DMT, Entheogenic Neurotransmitter*

Symptoms: Individuals with inflamed egos may exhibit any combination of the following behavioral patterns: tendency to religious, spiritual, or metaphysical beliefs of all kinds, passionate commitment to political ideologies, personal sense of identity intimately connected to culture, religion, ethnic group, or any subdivision of the universal category of "human being," tendency towards fear, self-doubt, judgment, hatred, attachment to any contrived sense of "purpose," criticism of self and/or others, addiction to interpersonal drama, sense of victimization, martyrdom, alienation, apathy, despair, separation, loneliness, nihilism, fatalism, dogmatism, fanaticism, fundamentalism, violence, manipulation, domination, exploitation, tendency towards fantasy and projection of self-generated illusions, regular suppression of true feelings, hesitancy to be oneself, etc.

Directions: Apply medicine directly to inflamed ego. Inflammation should disperse within 30 – 45 seconds. If ego inflammation persists, apply more medicine. Repeat as necessary as ego inflammation reoccurs.

Recommending Physician: *God*

The Entheological Paradigm: An Overview

From www.entheological-paradigm.net

Introduction:

This essay presents an overview to the Entheological Paradigm, a comprehensive map to the true nature of reality and how individuals can come to genuine knowledge of the self and the nature of God.

The ideas and arguments presented in the following rest on the fundamental understanding that human beings have both the *right* and *ability* to know themselves. Perhaps unexpectedly, the Entheological Paradigm articulates that the most genuine and effective path to self-awareness, personal liberation, and direct clarity into the true nature of reality is to be found through the use of entheogens, also known as hallucinogens and psychedelics.

Setting supposedly moral, political, social, and religious views aside, entheogens are simply tools for self-exploration and reflection: nothing more, and nothing less. The fact that they are largely illegal aptly demonstrates the deep level of fear of facing and knowing the self that exists in many modern societies. Ignorance is not bliss, however, and there are profound consequences for our unwillingness to face ourselves and the truth of our existence.

The Entheological Paradigm is here presented in overview in the hopes that rational dialogue and investigation can overcome the near-hysterical fears irrational laws present in many modern societies surrounding entheogens and their use. Rational, healthy societies could make profound use of these unique tools. Yet despite the fact the scientific evidence continually accumulates showing the benefits of these medicines, laws and social policy lag far behind, being largely reactionary and prejudicial, especially when the "spiritual" use of entheogens is taken into account.

The Entheological Paradigm points even beyond the therapeutic and "spiritual" use of entheogens and shows how their intentional use is actually necessary for full energetic awareness, which is here equated with direct, genuine experience of the true nature of reality. This is revolutionary and holds the potential to radically and permanently change the course of human history for it shows how it is fully possible for humanity to answer the fundamental questions of existence. The focus on "faith" and "belief" in religions and spiritual traditions are actually obsolete, as is atheism and pure scientific materialism. Entheogens make direct perception of reality available to anyone willing to do the necessary work and withstand the rigors of the experience. Everyone can experience this for him or herself. There is no longer a need to "believe" anything, and in fact, beliefs are exposed for exactly what they are in the process: beliefs, and not reality.

In the pages that follow, the Entheological Paradigm is presented as a coherent collection of ideas, positions, and experiential practices. For the most part, these ideas are presented matter-of-factly with little argumentation. Part of the power of these ideas is that, when taken as a whole, they make logical sense and can easily be accepted by those who approach them with an open mind and a willingness to consider what is genuinely and truly known about the nature of reality.

Readers may find that certain ideas make them very uncomfortable. Whenever such occurs, readers are encouraged to consider how the ideas presented here may conflict with their beliefs and on what grounds. Is there a belief there that could be let go of? What is served by holding onto that belief, and can that belief be confirmed by a consensus view of reality through rational exploration or investigation? Ultimately, a significant part of the process of fully opening to one's true nature is to undergo a process of "unlearning," as in the end, all beliefs are self-created energetic limitations that can be transcended through the simple act of making the choice to do so. The key, of course, is knowing how to actually make the choice and how that affects the individual energetically.

For a more thorough presentation of the Entheological Paradigm, readers are directed toward my book, *Being Human: An Entheological Guide to God, Evolution, and the Fractal Energetic Nature of Reality.*

The Basics:

While the Entheological Paradigm has some similarities to various religions, spiritual traditions, philosophies, and other worldviews, it is not a "belief" system and is in fact a comprehensive explanation for the fundamental, unitary, energetic nature of reality.

The Entheological Paradigm provides unprecedented clarity into what it means to be human, free from any metaphysical speculation, religious dogma, ego-generated illusion, and mythological thinking. It can be experienced directly by anyone who is willing to undergo the process of opening to their true energy and genuine nature with the guided use of entheogenic neurotransmitters.

The level of individual awareness and responsibility that the Entheological Paradigm provides is unprecedented in human history as it offers a direct and immediate route for each individual to directly experience and understand him or herself as an embodiment of God. Incomparable to any other method or technique, the Entheological Paradigm is fundamentally unique.

Reality

All of reality, including all life and consciousness, is the manifestation of a Unitary Energy Being. In simplest terms, everything that exists is God. There is nothing that is not God.

Reality, the physical and mental universe that we find ourselves in, is what God is "doing." Reality is an ongoing process of transformation of energy in the being that is God. God is the only being that exists. Reality is God's way of overcoming infinite unity: the imposition of energetic limits so that there might be multiplicity and experience. What we experience as limitations in physical reality are necessary for the energetic system of reality to function and evolve.

All of reality is energy, in one form or another. There is nothing that exists that is not a form of energy. Life and Consciousness are also forms of energy.

Energy

All energy continually transforms and interacts with other expressions of energy.

The nature of energy and the transformations of energy are mathematical in nature.

Mathematical permutations of energy take the forms of fundamental geometry (crystalline structures, basic geometric shapes) and fractal geometry (organic and inorganic meta-structures).

Both large-scale and small-scale structures, from quantum objects to DNA and river systems are fractal expressions.

Life and consciousness are also fractal expressions of energy and exhibit fundamental geometry as expressed through habitual behaviors, thought patterns, mannerisms, belief systems, and means of personal and individual expression.

All systems and spectrums of energy are united in the Unitary Energy Being, God. God is a fractal energy being that unifies all of reality through multiple energetic permutations of itself in infinite forms simultaneously.

Life and Consciousness

Living beings are direct embodiments of the Unitary Energy Being. Each individual life is a unique perspective of the One Being. Each individual is also completely autonomous and has free will to choose, within the energetic limits of reality.

Life and Consciousness are not mere accidental "by-products" of physical evolution. They are a fundamental energy that exist in the being of God and in fact are God.

God has been evolving all of reality through billions of years of energetic transformations in order to evolve increasingly complex and sophisticated bio-vehicles for it to experience reality with.

Human self-awareness and ability is the epitome of the evolution of the universe. It is the purpose of existence: God embodied in self-aware beings with the ability and capacity to understand their true place in existence and the physical ability to manipulate that reality and shape it according to choice.

However, humans are limited by their egos, the very function of consciousness that allows them to have true self-awareness. In order for humans to become genuinely aware embodiments of God, they must directly experience their true infinite nature as energetic beings. A full energetic opening coincides with ego transcendence.

The Role of Entheogens

Entheogenic substances are necessary tools for human beings to be able to fully perceive and experience their true energetic natures. Similar to the role of telescopes in astronomy, microscopes in microbiology and particle accelerators in quantum physics, human neurotransmitters such as DMT, and particularly 5-MeO-DMT, are necessary catalysts for human perception to fully open to energy.

Through the proper, guided and intentional use of entheogens, individuals can learn how to identify and accept their genuine energetic natures.

Opening to the reality of energy brings about transcendence of the ego, personal transformation, and ultimate liberation from all limiting belief systems, behavior patterns, and harmful modes of thought and action to self and others.

Entheogenic Evolution as Supra-Transcendental Evolution

Reality has moved through distinct evolutionary stages: inorganic, organic, transcendental evolution (human self-awareness and expression through religion, culture, arts, sciences, etc.), and supra-transcendental evolution (the transcendence of limited, egoic consciousness)

Through the use of entheogens, humans have the ability to come to direct knowledge of their true energetic natures, thereby transcending all religious, cultural, speculative, and illusory concepts of reality and self-identity as created by the ego.

When this can be accomplished on a large-scale, human evolution will catapult into the supra-transcendental stage where all religions, cultures, and divisive and contradictory belief systems will be transcended and human societies will enter into an unprecedented level of cooperation, unity, respect, and responsibility for the reality of our fundamental unity.

The next stage in evolution hinges on the conscious choice of individuals to let go of their illusions and resistance to the reality of being God in a body and take responsibility for who and what they truly are. The only way for this to occur is for individuals to embrace and take responsibility for their genuine energetic natures.

Belief Systems:

Liberation Through Unknowing

The Entheological Paradigm, while embracing and promoting a highly-revised and innovative understanding of God, is largely at odds with both traditional and New Age religious and spiritual views. Mystics have claimed throughout the ages that God is one, is within each individual and is, in some mystical sense, reality. Yet these insights have been obscured and wrapped in mystification, ritual, symbolism, and religious beliefs and cultural systems of identity. Unlike any other description of reality, The Entheological Paradigm is a work of systematic clarity with no mystification or positing of unseen realities.

The Entheological Paradigm therefore promotes "liberation through unknowning." Ultimately, all religious and spiritual beliefs are impediments to directly experiencing the fundamental energetic nature of reality in the present moment. All limiting and illusory beliefs must be transcended in order for reality to be experienced with clarity, liberated from all self-generated and ego-produced confusion.

The truth is that each individual living being is a direct embodiment of God, the Unitary Energy Being that is the source of all the energy in existence. Humans, as living beings, are unique expressions and embodiments of God for the fact that humans have self-awareness and egos - something that is largely absent in other living beings, with some rudimentary exceptions for apes and cetaceans. Because of this fact, humans have a unique capacity to awaken to their true identities as embodiments of the infinite energy being that is reality. To do so, they must learn how to energetically transcend their egos into full, infinite self-awareness through the guided use of entheogens.

Unlike most religious and spiritual traditions, The Entheological Paradigm promotes the distinct view that "this is it!" Reality, as we experience it as embodied beings in a "physical" universe is what is "real." There is nothing "beyond." Simply put, this is it. What we see is what we get.

Also unlike most religious and spiritual traditions, The Entheological Paradigm concludes that there are no intermediary realms, entities, or metaphysical energies between living beings and God: living beings are God directly in embodied form. In the case of humans, it is only the limiting energetic constructs of egoic-beliefs and projections that separate humans from awareness and acceptance of their true natures as embodiments of God.

The Entheological Paradigm promotes radical non-dualism. There is no separation. Any perception or experience of separation is self-generated and ultimately illusory.

The Basic Truth

The logic of the Entheological Paradigm is quite simple: God is a unitary energy being that is all of reality. The only thing that separates humans from their direct experience and acceptance of themselves as God is the energetic limitations created by their belief systems, which in turn influence the choices individuals make, how they choose to express themselves, and how they relate to the genuine and authentic energy that gives them life, awareness, experience, and being.

While religions and spiritual traditions have taught methods to transcend the ego, these methods have consistently been wrapped within ego-generated illusions of metaphysical realities, invisible spirits and energies, and numerous other wild and unsupported speculations that require adherence to practices of "liberation," "salvation," and "enlightenment". These beliefs separate individuals from their immediate energetic reality. Even when providing some extent of ego-transcendence, the belief systems themselves provide ample opportunity for egos to stay attached to illusions and cultural constructs, helping them to shape their identities and sense of self. Religions, at best, provide an expanded sense of self, but it is still limited from true energetic reality.

The only truly effective method for both transcending all belief systems as well as simultaneously opening an individual's ability to perceive and experience energy, the fundamental nature of reality, is the careful, guided, and intentional use of entheogens, especially 5-MeO-DMT, a natural neurotransmitter found in every mammal and every human being.

Energetics:

Understanding Fundamental Reality

The key concept of the Entheological Paradigm is that of "energy." Everything that exists is a form of energy. While many religions and spiritual traditions make similar, if not identical claims, empirical, physical and mathematical sciences have done a superior job in producing genuine, culture-free knowledge of reality and the true nature of energetic systems. This is due to the scientific emphasis on measurement and observation. Reality is made out of math, and all expressions of energy have mathematical qualities. When given shape in space and time, these mathematical permutations of energy evolve into fractal forms, constituting the perceivable universe.

Energetic systems are fractal systems. Fractal mathematics can describe everything from quantum physics to the shape of DNA, the branches on a tree, the veins in our bodies, the rivers that cross the land, the clouds that grace the sky, to the vast forms of cosmic gas that float through space.

All of reality is one vast, infinitely complex, energetic system.

A Living Universe

Yet is it not just a "dead," "physical" system. While the Entheological Paradigm is largely in agreement with the empirical, physical, and mathematical sciences, it is far more encompassing in its scope of energetic reality. Grand Unified Theories in physics, for example, have no account or explanation for the existence of life and consciousness in a supposedly purely "physical" system. The Entheological Paradigm is a true Grand Unified Theory for it accepts the unique energy of life and consciousness as not being a mysterious "by-product" of the universe, but rather as a fundamental energy of reality. In short, reality is itself a conscious, self-aware, living being. That being is God: The Unitary Energy Being. That being replicates itself in countless energetic forms simultaneously and is the very life and consciousness that finds expression in each individual living being. God is the very energy of existence and life itself.

God is a Fractal Energy Being that continually replicates itself through evolution within a universe of its own creation in order for there to be a genuine arena in which the exercise of free will, or conscious choice, by autonomous individuals, is an experiential reality.

Enactment of choice is an expression of energy. Choices that align with the true energy of reality are harmonious. Choices that are out of alignment with true reality (choices based on illusions or false beliefs) cause suffering as there is resistance between the agent making the choice and the genuine energy of reality. Religious beliefs are almost universally out of alignment with genuine energetic reality in that they posit numerous imaginary constructs: souls, an afterlife, reincarnation, etc. Choices based on religious beliefs are therefore almost always trapped in egoic constructs that are fundamentally untrue.

The Human Energetic System

In the simplest terms, a human being is a perfect bio-vehicle for God to enjoy reality in. Through the evolution of living beings over countless eons, the Unitary Energy Being that is reality has been developing more and more sophisticated bio-vehicles. This is the nature of energetic evolution: systems become more complex and sophisticated over time.   Energetic systems are expressions of interlacing mathematical patterns that build on earlier transformations of energy.

As an energetic system, the evolution of life has reached an energetic breakthrough in humanity: bio-vehicles with sufficiently sophisticated nervous systems and the mental capacity to become self-aware (something largely lacking from the rest of biological life). Thus the evolutionary energetic construct of the ego developed in human consciousness to facilitate the process of awakening to self-awareness.

The ego, however, is ultimately an illusory construct. Given that all life and reality is, in truth, one, the egoic perspective of being an individual being among others in a universe that is fundamentally separate from the self is a sophisticated illusion. It is necessary for the evolution of self-awareness, but it is still an illusion.

When the ego is transcended through energetic opening to one's true nature, reality can be directly experienced as one, interconnected, vastly complex, living being.   The surprise for the ego is that YOU ARE THAT BEING. There is no separation - only the illusion of separation. And that being is clearly not the ego, or what the ego thinks of as its self.

The inevitable conclusion, the simple truth that all humans must simply accept, is that each individual is God. We are all one being, multiplied out into innumerable autonomous versions of itself.

As bio-vehicles for God, humans have three primary energy centers that power their vehicle directly from source. These three centers are consciousness as physically manifested through the brain, sensory organs, and nervous system, life energy/love as manifested through the heart, lungs, and vascular system, and the energy of creation as manifested through the sexual organs and gonads and as given greatest expression in procreation.

As individual vehicles, humans also have the energy center of their central core as individual physical beings, which is comprised of the throat and stomach/digestive tract. Our throat is our energetic input/output mechanism that allows us to intake from reality (food and nourishment) as well as express ourselves and our minds through sound, expression, and language. What we do with our input/output mechanism affects the digestive tract and influences how we are processing reality.

How we choose to think, feel, love, act, and express ourselves is our engagement with the energy that is our life. When our choices are energetically in alignment with reality, we live in harmony and truth. When our choices are out of alignment, we feel energetically disturbed. We feel fearful, judgmental, irrational, jealous, cynical, hopeless, hated and hateful.

Physical, biological beings are energy beings. Our bodies run on electromagnetic energy. The source of all life and energy is one. We are liquid crystalline beings, animated by energy that permeates the holographic grid of our fractal DNA, giving our life and consciousness expression in physical form.

If all living beings are embodiments of the one energy being, then what makes humans so special? The answer is that our capacity for expression, communication, and manipulation and understanding of our physical environment far surpasses any other life form. For this reason, humans are the most capable of expressing God's infinite nature of all the bio-vehicles God has to enjoy and experience reality in. Humans, of all living beings, have the greatest capacity for the expression of free will and choice.

Because humans are the most sophisticated bio-vehicles for God, they also bear the greatest responsibility for themselves and how they choose to shape their world, both internally and externally, and their interactions with others.

Our choices affect us energetically. Choices that deny or conflict with our fundamental energy do us damage physically, emotionally, and mentally. Such choices also increase the likelihood that one will inflict harm and suffering on others as well.

Clarity in who one is and what one's energy is produces harmonious experience for the self and for others.

The Work:

Opening to Energy with Entheogens

The basic truth that each individual human being is God in a body, yet most are largely unaware of this fact and even if "believed," is still not practically understood, necessitates a methodology for discovering, accepting, and embodying this fundamental truth of our existence.

Given that God is an energy being, to be able to fully experience oneself as God means that one must learn to process, perceive, experience, and work with the true energy of one's being. Religious and spiritual traditions have developed various methods for deepening one's perception and awareness of oneself, and have even developed energetic methodologies and teachings. The problem is that these teachings almost inevitably involve concepts of "subtle" energy, "subtle bodies," and unseen, mystical forces. These teachings are also wrapped in complex symbolism, mythology, and esoteric systems of personal "liberation," often pointing to the "true reality" as being anywhere but the actual reality that we all collectively inhabit on planet Earth.

For example, in Eastern traditions such as Buddhism and Hinduism, there is the teaching of the "chakra" system: a series of "invisible" energy centers both within and outside of our physical bodies. Practitioners are taught how to "visualize" and "access" these energy centers. While producing energetic experiences, this is ultimately an imaginary system. No scientist or doctor will ever be able to find or detect your chakras because they don't exist. Furthermore, these energetic teachings are based in a belief system of reincarnation and the need for ultimate "liberation" from this process of death and rebirth. This is an entirely erroneous concept as each living being is already God. There is only one being, so concepts of personal reincarnation are baseless and illusory.

Shamanic energy work does not fare any better. While many shamans work directly with energy, they also work with dis-incarnate entities, spirits, and "other worlds." Though effective, to some extent, working with spirits is ultimately working with illusions and projections in the Divine Imagination (explained below). Remember: The Entheological Paradigm teaches that all biological, living beings are God - they do not have "spirits" and there are no other "realms" with "living" beings in non-biological forms.

So how can one encounter one's energy and learn to work with it unburdened by imaginary belief systems and illusions?

The answer is simple: entheogens.

Entheogens are "substances that generate the experience of God within." Many religions and shamanic traditions have made use of entheogens, but the methodology of the Entheological Paradigm is unique from these previous entheogenic practices and therefore presents a new system of direct, immediate experience to humanity.

Direct and Immediate Clarity

5-MeO-DMT, a natural neurotransmitter that is found in every mammal and every human, has played an important role in both mammalian evolution and human consciousness. Present in the human nervous system, this neurotransmitter regulates the human ability to perceive and experience extremely fine levels of energetic vibrations. When small amounts (10-20 mg) of this crystalline compound is consumed from an outside source, it produces an almost instantaneous shift in ability to perceive and experience energy. The experience of energy is so profound, in fact, that it almost demands a full surrender of the ego, releasing the individual into a fully expanded energetic state, if the individual can choose to completely let go. It is highly significant to recognize that "letting go" completely into one's energy is always a matter of free choice. It is always possible for resistant individuals to attempt to "keep a grip" on their illusions and structured sense of self, unwilling to release the death grip of the ego on one's personal perspective.

The radical and immediate perceptual shift afforded by ingestion of 5-MeO-DMT is incomparable to any other method or tool available to humanity. For those who are ready to accept what they experience, it is the greatest possible clarity into the true nature of one's being. It is direct, immediate, and obviously the fundamental nature of reality and one's being. It is the fullest energetic experience of being God in a body that humans are capable of achieving.

Traditional meditation and energetic practices as taught by religions and spiritual traditions are of a far lower order of magnitude than the 5-MeO-DMT experience. While "mystical" experiences of "union" with God have been known throughout history, the full energetic opening occasioned by ingestion of 5-MeO-DMT is a direct and immediate immersion in full energetic reality that is incomparable in nature and perfect clarity.

Given that 5-MeO-DMT is a compound that anyone could potentially consume for their own personal exploration and self-transcendence, it renders religious and spiritual traditions obsolete. Every human being already is God: they just need a crystal key to unlock their ability to perceive and experience themselves as such. Spiritual paths and religious dogmas are simply no longer relevant.

Working With the Medicines

There are a variety other entheogenic compounds that allow for direct openings to one's genuine energy. 5-MeO-DMT provides the fullest, most expanded experience, but DMT follows a close second. For the most rewarding and productive entheogenic work, these are the two compounds that are most useful for human development. Both are natural human neurotransmitters and therefore, while occasioning deeply expanded experiences of great complexity and beauty, are very natural for human use as there is nothing "foreign" about their chemistry. In fact, they are among the few compounds that are so readily accepted by our brains that they almost instantly cross the blood/brain barrier when consumed.

Working with entheogens is a unique methodology that, if used properly, can achieve the following results for dedicated individuals:

- Removal of energetic blocks and patterns of resistance
- Transcend the ego and habitual patterns of behavior and thought
- Purge energy stored from fear, judgment, illusion
- Release attachment to illusory beliefs and self-created delusions
- Expand fully into one's true energetic state
- Perceive and experience the fundamental energetic unity of all things
- Perceive and experience the fundamental unity of all life and consciousness
- Heal traumatic experiences and release energetic residue
- Achieve personal clarity into one's true nature
- Take responsibility for all of one's choices
- Understand the nature of free will and conscious choice
- Discover one's true energetic core
- Learn authentic expression and speaking in absolute truth
- Harmonize one's inner relationship with oneself and thereby all beings
- Liberation from all personal imaginary limitations

The above benefits are achieved when individuals relax completely into their experience. It is best for individuals to keep their postures energetically open in order to experience the most relaxed state. This means lying back with legs slightly open and knees slightly bent. Arms should be kept at the sides with palms up and hands open. This posture communicates "I am open and willing to receive whatever comes during my experience."

Unlike mystical and shamanic traditions that teach that one's consciousness can enter into other planes of existence and communicate with mysterious, mystical spirits and beings, the Entheological Paradigm holds that all such experiences are best understood as manifestations of the Divine Imagination. The Divine Imagination is an energetic state of perception and experience that is ultimately a mirror reflection of the individual's perspective. The Divine Imagination is like an interactive, multi-dimensional virtual reality that is projected from our own energy and there is nothing within it that is not the self, in some form or another. It is a highly sophisticated, interactive mirror.

The clearest experiences of the Divine Imagination occur with high-level entheogenic experiences where the fundamental, underlying energy of reality is perceived and experienced directly as the self. This is the clearest reflection in the mirror of the Divine Imagination. At high levels of DMT, for example, individuals experience themselves as startlingly complex arrays of intricate geometric patterns, grids, and energetic architecture. This is a clear reflection of our fractal/geometric energetic natures as the One Energy Being: God.

However, since it is an imaginative experience, the fundamental energetic geometry can appear to one in any variety of forms from entities to landscapes, complex architecture, scenes and vistas, and encounters with seemingly very real beings. Many of these visionary experiences can be very revealing to individuals, especially when they are appreciated for what they are: reflections of the self.

Part of the process of working with entheogens for the purpose of full energetic awakening is learning to accept all that one experiences are manifestations of the self, no matter how "other" or alien the experiences may seem. The simple truth is that for one who is clear and centered in their energy, not even the strongest entheogen can remove them from being immediately present and focused. Those who know who and what they are are not caught by illusions or flights of thought.

Working in an Ego-Suspended State

When sufficient quantities of entheogens are consumed so that the practitioner can reach a "full release" state, the ego can be transcended. The ultimate goal of practice is to learn to maintain one's center in an ego-transcended state and be fully present at all times, not just when working with entheogens. But learning what this actually means takes time and practice with the medicines. Because operating from a fully energetically open state is so fundamentally distinct from "normal" human action and interaction, it must first be learned with the assistance of the entheogenic medicines. Once one is sufficiently familiar with the practice and the experiential state of being liberated from the ego, then full integration of the experience with everyday life and consciousness becomes possible. When this is achieved, a person has successfully self-liberated themselves from the confines of their ego and are able to live in the energetic truth of reality.

Entheogenic experiences can be described as an arc of ego transcendence, which takes its most dramatic form when working with powerful tryptamines such as DMT and 5-MeO-DMT. In the first few instants, the ego has the choice to struggle to hold on, or release in surrender and trust. If the ego fails to release, it will use whatever "tricks" have served it best to keep the individual's consciousness locked into self-projection. Some will use fear, others "thinking too much." The ego will grasp at whatever tools it has found useful in the past.

When the ego lets go, however, the individual enters into an open energetic state. At this point individuals generally begin to be moved by their authentic energy. If they need to release deep energy, they may purge, scream, cry, or any other similar, forceful manners of releasing. It is quite common for individuals to find many subsequent layers of energy to release and let go of.

Resisting the flow of energy can create vibrations throughout the body. When this occurs, vibrations can be minimized by consciously relaxing and returning to the open body posture described above. Vibrations can also serve to clear out blocks in the body and open up areas in your being where your current might be weak or constricted.

When individuals are truly relaxed and centered, they begin to move spontaneously in mirrored symmetrical movements that coincide with the bilateral symmetry of their bodies. In such states individuals always maintain a center line down the middle of their body such that their two hands might meet together, but hands will not cross to the opposite side of the body.

Many individuals also begin to spontaneously vocalize. The purest forms of vocalizations in such states are generally pure tones, throat and overtone singing, and other vibratory noises. Glossolalia, or "speaking in tongues," is generally a sign that someone is trying too hard and their ego is intervening.

Eventually the ego will begin to reassert itself and an individual might find themselves asking themselves what it is that they are doing or why they are moving about and making the sounds that they are. These are the first glimmers of egoic self-consciousness. If one chooses, one can continue to let go of the ego at this point and continue the experience. This is a learned skill, however, and generally as soon as the ego can reassert itself, it will, and the individual will return to "normal" egoic consciousness.

The goal of such practices is to allow the individual to learn to recognize and trust their own innate energy. In the entheogenic state, they will feel "inspired" by their energy. They will learn how it directs their body, their thoughts, their feelings and their very life. They can then learn to recognize how the choices they make, especially how they choose to react to situations and events and in their relationships with others and themselves, bring them either into or out of alignment with their innate flow of energy.

What this fundamentally boils down to is learning how to live in the truth of one's genuine energy. One then learns how to be responsible for oneself - the only person anyone can every truly be responsible for. One learns to how be truthful with themselves and with all aspects of their life, bringing them into greater and greater harmony with their highest expression of themselves as an embodiment of the One Being.

Opening to one's energy with entheogens is a demanding, yet profoundly rewarding, process. Truly opening to energy requires letting go of all preconceptions and willingness to surrender in trust to your life force and the energy of all that is. This is not work that should be taken lightly. It is powerful and transformative.

Trusting your energy means being able to trust the flow of your life and trusting the energy of your heart. You have embraced yourself fully and you know that there is nothing in your energy to fear. You live in the truth of your being and you live in genuine reality, unencumbered by self-generated illusion.

The Fruits:

Liberation for All

The fruits of doing the work to open to one's energy and true nature with entheogens are many. In truth, it is nothing short of genuine human liberation. In the most practical terms, when one has learned how to recognize and accept one's true energy and transcend the ego, then an individual can simply be him or herself, fully, completely, and authentically.

This is the ultimate goal of the Entheological Paradigm: helping people become themselves in their genuine, fully energetically open form. The goal is to be fully human.

As surprising as it may seem, people are honestly confused about what it means to be human, and are especially confused about what it means to truly be themselves. This is for a variety of reasons, but much of the problem boils down to culture, identity, and belief systems. All humans are born into a family, culture, ethnic group, religion, tradition, and other systems of belief, practice, and worldviews. Individuals are shaped by the context in which they find themselves. All belief systems, however, are constructs of culture, as are the behavior patterns that grow from these belief systems.

Constructs, while communicative, meaningful, and shared among collections of individuals to produce group affirmation of experience and interpretation, are not necessarily reality. They are constructs. The difference between reality and a construct is that reality is how things are, not how they might be, nor how they might be otherwise. Culture is always "how things might be otherwise," for another culture, religion, or tradition, could always "do it differently" and have completely contradictory values, beliefs, and understandings. Genuine, True Reality is made of limits that must be accepted because we cannot choose for things to be otherwise. Cultures, by contrast, are largely collections of relative choices.

Any human being could potentially be raised in any religion, culture, or identity group. Anyone can potentially take on the beliefs, experiences, and patterns of any system. The human potential for variety is infinite. Each system presents options for choices and evaluations for human action and thought. Each system has its own version of what it means to be human, and also what it means to be a good or bad, successful or unsuccessful, human. Yet virtually all such constructs are relative. They are not fundamentally true. For this reason, culture (religion, tradition, belief system) is inherently limiting for any given individual as it arbitrarily limits the individual's true, infinite nature. To accomplish this, the culture or tradition needs to convince the ego to internalize the beliefs, values, and systems of thought and practice, thereby shaping the identity of the individual. The effect is universal and comprehensive: confused, self-limiting individuals who cause their own unnecessary suffering and bring suffering to others, especially those who are considered "not us" or "other."

Liberation into the true energetic nature of the self and one's being through entheogens bypasses all cultural constructs and belief systems, particularly at high levels of energetic opening and experience. It is immediate experience that transcends all imposed limits that have been accepted by the ego. It is the complete transcendence of egoic identity.

Encounters with the True Self

Through practice while in an open energetic state, individuals learn how to recognize and accept their genuine energy, liberated from the constructs of culture, tradition, and belief systems. It is this experience that allows an individual to perceive genuine truth, unencumbered by arbitrary limitations. The individual learns to recognize the truth of the energy of his or her being in the present moment. Freed from all projections and ego games, the moment of now unfolds into infinity, revealing the unity of all things.

Recognition of the unified nature of reality and the center of the self is the beginning of trust. Trust brings about greater relaxation, confidence, and enjoyment of life and all moments. The present moment becomes the true focus of one's attention and life, for it is here, now, in this very moment that the energy of your life is continually transforming and responding to all the energies around it. You see how your choices, every choice, in every moment, guide the unfolding of your life. Living in honesty, truth, and all that is genuine and real becomes the foremost concern in one's life. Being present. Being here. Being human. Being yourself.

In the end, this is the only purpose of existence: for each individual to fully and completely be him or herself. Human beings, because we are so thoroughly cultural animals, have the greatest difficulty in discovering and trusting in who we truly are. The meta-structures of culture, tradition, religion, and belief systems have provided for continuity of societies and ways of life, but the time has now come where humans are ready to transcend the arbitrary limits they have placed on themselves. The time has come for people to truly be who they are: full embodiments of God, with infinite potential to live harmoniously and gloriously in reality. None of us need to be saved. None of us need to escape the wheel of rebirth. None of us need to purify ourselves. None of us need to deny who or what we truly are for imaginary egoic projections and illusions. We only need to be ourselves fully, in every moment, and live with each other in the honest recognition of reality.

Liberation into Truth and Reality

Humanity has been in its infancy. Cultures have told themselves countless stories about themselves and the universe, giving meaning to their existence and satisfying their true desire to know and understand. Through altered states of consciousness, humans have always experienced the fantastical, otherworldly, the terrifying and the sublime. Yet when genuine empirical investigations into nature revealed no such genuine realities, the Divine Imagination was exposed for what it is: an imaginative experience. Complex, paradoxical, beyond "normal" human imagination, but imagination, nevertheless. A sophisticated way humanity has been interacting with itself as both perceiver and that which is perceived.

Now humanity has found a method to reach genuine consensus about the nature of reality through empirical, mathematical, sciences. Particle physics and astrophysics are genuine knowledge about the energetic structures and systems of reality. There are no angels, divine beings, or ascended masters out there: just infinite amounts of energy. It doesn't take a ritual or a prayer to log onto the internet or make your computer work. You don't have to "believe" in technology for it to work because it is based on knowledge that is true: precise, mathematical knowledge of energy and energetic systems.

And when we look within, with clarity and honesty, we find that there is only the "I." And what is that "I" that flows in a torrent of infinite energy that unites and unifies all things in one vast, interconnected network of energy? If there is nothing between you and that infinite energy, then all separation is merely illusion.

It is you.

It is I.

It is God.

To be God is to be liberated from all ego games of illusion and suffering. It is to live in truth and accept the full reality of one's life.

And the reality is that from this perspective, you are a human life, a human being. You are God, but you are also God as embodied in a human bio-vehicle. Only you can liberate yourself into genuine awareness of who and what you are. The responsibility is 100% yours and yours alone.

Human life is short. The time each individual has is limited. True liberation awaits YOU. NOW.

The Process
An Experiential Discourse on
Unitary Being

Introduction:

"The Process" is the transcript from an episode of *The Entheogenic Evolution* Podcast on 4/16/10 (www.entheogenic.podomatic.com). For this episode, I spoke directly to the listeners while energetically expanded and in full unitary consciousness. After I first "broke open" back in the Spring of 2009, I put out a number of podcast episodes concerning the Entheological Paradigm and explaining all that I had learned from my transformation. There came a point where I decided that I had said all that I needed to say, and as I was mostly no longer interested in interviewing others, I stopped putting out new episodes of the podcast. However, in the Spring of 2010, I felt up to giving a demonstration, of sorts, and "The Process" was the result.

The term, "the process," is meant to indicate the multi-layered nature of existence as an ongoing, continual transformation. This applies both to "exterior" reality as well as our own direct experience of becoming, and the nature of undergoing personal awakening into the true self. It is all "the process." To truly be at peace, one must submit to the process.

I've experimented with placement of words on the page for this piece to capture something of the energetic nature of the original experience. I spoke in full "Voice" for this recording, and at times was vocalizing tones and vibrations, which aren't captured here. The poetic/stylistic rendering is meant to help express this. For anyone wanting the full experience, "The Process" is still available on the *Entheogenic Evolution* podcast.

Greetings, my friends.
Today I would like to talk to you about *The Process*.

Ah, *The Process. . . The Process. . . The Process* is all that exists. *The Process* is all that has ever been. *The Process* is all that there will be. There is nothing that exists that is not part of *The Process*. *The Process* is *All Things*. *You* are *The Process*.

You see, from your perspective, this is something that always holds true. You are the center of *The Process*. It all revolves around you. Doesn't it? Have you ever noticed that? Everything in *The Process* revolves around you. *You* are *The Process*.

From the center of *The Process* is the perspective of I Am . . . I Am . . . I Am.

I Am Myself. I Am the Center of *The Process*. All things that exist are part of *The Process*. My body is part of *The Process*. My ego - my sense of identity - that, too, is part of *The Process*.

Yet they are parts of *The Process*. They are manifestations of *The Process*. They are temporary configurations of *Energy* within *The Process*. Bodies come and go. Egos come and go. Identities come and go. *The Process* continues.

I Am . . . I Am . . . I Am . . .

The Process continues . . .

Within *The Process*, there are billions of perspectives. Yet within each perspective, I Am.

In every perspective, I Am.

In every perspective, I Am.

In every perspective, I Am.

No matter where I stand, my perspective is the Center of *The Process*. No matter where I find myself, my perspective is the Center of *The Process*, for I Am *The Process*. *The Process* is all that exists. It is all that there has ever been, and it is all that there ever shall be.

The Process is *Now*!

The Process is this very moment NOW!

It is NOW.

It is the eternal unfolding of NOW.

THIS is The Process.

I Am *The Process.* There is nothing that is not part of *The Process.* There is nothing that is not myself. I Am all things. I Am all that there has ever been, and I Am all that there will ever be . . .

For I Am the Eternal Moment of NOW. I Am *The Process.*

And that is true from every perspective. This is the **Truth** that is found at the Center of Every Perspective.

I AM.

I AM.

So we begin with that truth, that fundamental truth of *The Process.* That truth is that I am. I exist and I am *The Process.* There is nothing that is separate.

There is only One.

There is only One.

There is only One . . .

And   this   is   **T r u e**   for   *Every   Perspective.*

So then, what is *The Process*?

What is It? . . . What is It? . . . What is It? . . . What is It? . . .

What am I? . . . What is It?

What is the difference between I and It? Is there a difference between I and It?

I Am It.

It is I. It is the Self.

The Self is a *game*.

The Process is a game, for within *The Process* there is only One, yet so many perspectives, so many bodies, so many infinite versions of the Self all participating together within *The Process*, which is One.

So many perspectives, all at once, together.

So many that are One.

One and Many, One and Many, One and Many.

We Are.

We Are.

We Are here together.

We Are here in The One, together . . . Together, for there is One . . .

And there are Many . . .

The Game.

The game of Self and Other. Subject and Object. Self and Not-Self.

To play the game it takes space and time. The Eternal Unfolding of *The Process*.

Time . . . time . . . time . . .

It has taken very, very long for *The Process* to reach the point where it is now.

Space and time needed to unfold and transform for a very long time, across infinite expanses of space in order to bring the multiplicity that is the One to the point of NOW.

Here.

Now.

You are *The Process.*

You are the center of *The Process.* You have always been the center of *The Process*, for there is nothing that is not you.

There is nothing that is not you.

So NOW

the *Time has Come*!

The time has come to awaken to WHO YOU ARE and take responsibility for yourself.

You are the Center of *The Process.*

You.

Yes!

You.

It is YOU!

Do not look to another. Do not look outside of yourself, for it is you.

You are It.

It is You.

You!

You are all that there has ever been.

You   are   all   that   there   will   ever   be.

So, how are you playing the game?

What is your part in *The Process*?

Yes?

Yes?

Have you found your center?

If you are living in your ego then you have no idea who you are.

Only when you can find your center, will you know the perspective of the true self.

Only then will you understand your place within *The Process*; only when you find your center. To find your center you must look within.

Do not look for Me anywhere but the Center of the Self, for that is where I Am.

Where else would I Be but at the Center of All Things?

Understand that I am you.

You are Me.

We are One.

There is *no separation*.

So many perspectives.

Only One.

Only One,
            One,
                        One,
                                    ONE!

Energy.

You are *Energy.*

I am *Energy.*

Each individual is responsible for how energy flows through his or her physical being. Every being is self-responsible for their own energy flow.

  Choice.
        Choice.
              Choice.

We choose and by our choices we construct *The Process* around our sense of self.

We choose.

We choose and by our choices we create. We create and we respond to what we create.

So be responsible.

Be responsible for yourself, for your energy, for your awareness, for the choices that you make, for you are the Center of *The Process.* How you choose will shape your reality, for *You* are *That.*

It is You.

There is no separation.

Many choices have already been made.

Many choices are far deeper than can be undone by any new choice.

These choices are what we call REALITY:

     To be Here, Now, in a *Body*,

         To breathe the *Air*,

             To feel the *Sunlight*,

                 To feel the *Ground* beneath my feet,

                     To see the *Stars* above my head.

To be here now many choices have already been made, and these choices can never be undone, for they are fundamental to the nature of *The Process*.

So the parameters of reality are established. They cannot be undone. They cannot be wished away. They cannot be willed away.

But they are you, so you can trust these choices, for you have already made them.

The rest is up to you.

>
> You are here.
>
> You are in your body.
>
> You are your life.
>
> You are your perspective.
>
> You are your choices.

You are everything that you will ever experience.

You are everything that you have ever known, and you are everything that you will ever be.

>
> It is all You.

So take responsibility, my friends.

Take responsibility for yourself here, now, in this body, in this time, in this life.

Take responsibility for who and what you are.

Take responsibility for what you are doing.

Take responsibility for what you are creating.

Take responsibility for how you choose to think of yourself.

Take responsibility for who you think you are.

Yes!

Who are You?

Look into the mirror of being. Look into the mirror of yourself. Look into the mirror of your life and see who you are.

What you believe is irrelevant.

What you think is irrelevant.

The Process is all that matters. *The Process* is all that exists. *The Process* is all that there has ever been. *The Process* is all there ever will be.

What you believe about *The Process* is irrelevant.

What you think about *The Process* is irrelevant.

The Process is not *personal.*

To find your place within *The Process*, don't take it personally.

What your ego thinks of *The Process* is irrelevant.

To find your place within *The Process*, set your ego aside.

It's simple.

Do it!

Set it aside.

. . . Ah, do you see?

It does not matter what you believe. It does not matter what you think.

It is what you Feel . . .

Energy

The nature of being.

Love.

That's all that there is.

Love.

The Process is love.

     The Process is love.

          The Process is love.

               The Process is love.

                    The Process is love.

Love. I Am Love. I Am Love. I Am Love.

Love. Love. Love. Love. Love. Love. Love. Love. Love. Love. LOVE!

THERE IS NOTHING ELSE!

Love. Love. Love. Love. Love. Love. Love. Love. Love. Love. LOVE!

Trust.

Within the self there is nothing to fear.

There is only love.

Trust.

Trust *The Process*.

Trust yourself.

Trust love.

Trust love. Love trust. Trust love. Love trust. Trust love. Love trust.

I/You, You/I, I/You, You/I, I/You, You/I
Trust Love, Love Trust, Trust Love, Love Trust
I/You, You/I, I/You, You/I, I/You, You/I
Trust Love, Love Trust, Trust Love, Love Trust

TRUST LOVE!

Terence on DMT
An Entheological Analysis of McKenna's Experiences in the Tryptamine Mirror of the Self

Introduction:

     In the late Spring of 2010, I made the following essay available for download via my account at Scribd.com. Within hours, it had been reposted at a psychedelic discussion forum and was already making readers very upset. A couple weeks later, it was published at RealitySandwich.com, where it found an even larger, and even more hostile, audience. Many readers seem to have taken my analysis of Terence McKenna very personally and harsh criticism ensued in ample measure. The article received numerous critical comments, though many focused more on personal attacks on me than the substance of the analysis that I provided. Discussions were also started at various forums on the web, and though some comments were in favor of my analysis and my work, the majority were not.

     In writing this piece, I didn't expect to make many friends. My intention was to stir things up, get people thinking, and expose egoic attachments and projections. Well, I accomplished that in spades! I knew that this would anger people, but I've made the decision to not censor myself or what I have to share based on how others may receive me, what I share, or how I choose to go about sharing it. My primary goal is to be myself, always. I was highly inspired to write this piece as it provided an opportunity to use the Entheological Paradigm to analyze the ideas of a widely-known "psychonaut" and present a radically different interpretation of the DMT experience. My interest is to help bring clarity to others, and this seemed like an efficient route for plantings seeds of clarity into what is otherwise a very confused portrait of DMT, 5-MeO-DMT, and the nature of the psychedelic experience in general. Though it is not a popular view, in my analysis, Terence McKenna's speculations about DMT are simply misguided and ultimately not helpful for understanding the nature of the self or reality in general.

As someone who has done a great deal of speaking and writing publicly about DMT and 5-MeO-DMT, I have been asked about my views on Terence and machine elves numerous times. In general, I've found that others have assumed that I "believe" in alternate realms, alien beings, and machine elves, and many are simply incredulous when I explain otherwise. The assumption is so strong that many apparently don't hear when I explain that all such entities are products of the ego and reflections of the individual, which always comes prior to question and answer period of my public speaking. I've also received emails from people asking what they're doing "wong," given that their own experiences haven't included "beings," "realms," and "machine elves". Furthermore, I've been asked to review manuscripts that recount other individuals' quests to encounter machine elves. Given the preponderance of such views, I decided that addressing the question directly and publicly was the most efficient route to begin to dispel the illusions of beings and realms.

Those who reacted to this article commonly claimed that I am arrogant, intolerant, and seriously lacking in humility. In many respects, these accusations are correct. In embracing my true energy, I've found that things like humility and tolerance are ego-driven values – manipulative tools that egos use to get others to reaffirm their illusions and projections - as well as desires to be accepted and liked by others (again, the ego seeking reaffirmation). Being genuine to myself and my energy means communicating authentically, and I'm not shy about telling it like it is, regardless of how others think. As I see it, this is the greatest gift I can give to others: genuine clarity.

Clarity is often confrontational, however, in that it confronts others with their own attachments and illusions and challenges those things with which one has constructed a sense of identity. I often say that dealing with me is like dealing with a dose of medicine: my approach can quickly expose discomfort, attachment, and projection within others, as not only is the information that I'm presenting challenging, but how I go about presenting it is a challenge as well.

Something that added to readers' frustration was the fact that I chose not to respond directly to any of the attacks and critiques that others were posting on-line. To many, this made me appear even more arrogant than before, as I was ignoring them. Again, this is largely true. In my experience, people who genuinely want to converse with me will contact me directly. Those who post their views on-line have largely already made up their minds and are most often working directly from their egos, especially when they are emotionally invested in the issue. Web forums do not provide for a genuine discussion, but they do provide a great space for people to get flared up. In short, I don't find forums fruitful, so I chose not to engage.

I'm presenting the essay here just as it was published previously. As readers of this book will see, everything that is mentioned here is in complete coherence with everything else I'm presenting about the Entheological Paradigm. If you're a fan of Terence, I advise you not to take this personally, and keep an open mind. Terence was friendly and entertaining. It doesn't mean that he really understood what he was talking about, however, and in the end, I completely stand behind the analysis presented here.

The Essay:

A name that is intimately tied to DMT (dimethyltryptamine), machine elves, aliens, and 2012 in the popular imagination is Terence McKenna. Though now deceased, Terence's musings on DMT continue to influence countless explorers of altered states of consciousness and his writings and lectures have left an indelible mark on popular psychedelic culture. Largely through the internet, Terence's accounts of his DMT experiences are now easily accessible and are posted and reposted throughout the cyber realms, where he is largely presented as a heroic explorer and radical thinker, challenging us all to embrace a profoundly enlarged view of reality; namely as experienced through DMT.

Are Terence and his wild accounts of DMT and machine elves all that they are made out to be? Is Terence a ground-breaking and reality-shattering explorer of the far realms of the psychedelic universe? Is he a torch-bearer leading us to a grander vision of all that *just might be?* Many seem to be convinced that the answer to these questions is an emphatic and undeniable "Yes!" despite the obvious reservations of more "rational" and "traditional" thinkers. Indeed, it is often the radical ontological and epistemological shift implied in accepting Terence's accounts that attract many "counter-cultural" thinkers and self-styled explorers of consciousness. It would be suspect if Terence's ideas were in conformity with the dominant paradigm and it is his image as an outsider and free-thinker that makes Terence so appealing to many and why they are so eager to absorb his reflections on his arguably quite strange DMT experiences.

I find Terence's reflections on his DMT experiences to be valuable and insightful for a very different reason. When analyzed from the perspective of what I call "The Entheological Paradigm," Terence's experiences do not present us with an intrepid explorer discovering new realms. Rather, we are presented with a clear picture of an individual who is unable to recognize himself in the mirror of tryptamine consciousness. In short, Terence's experiences boil down to one fundamental truth: they are the experiences of someone who is consuming very powerful entheogens yet is failing to recognize the projections and creations of his own ego while in that state. From the perspective of unitary consciousness, Terence appears to have never managed to transcend his ego and therefore appears to have failed to realize the genuinely true potential of the entheogenic medicines he chose to ingest.

When this perspective is understood, it becomes immediately clear that virtually *all* of what Terence has to say about DMT experiences are projections of his own ego. Terence has not explored some other realm or brought back valuable information for other would-be explorers, as he imagined himself doing: he has explored the confused projections of his own ego and never achieved anything close to clarity about those experiences. Ultimately, Terence brought us all back deep and abiding confusion, and his confusion has subsequently been eagerly and whole-heartedly embraced by countless others in the entheogenic community. For the information that Terence brought back to us to be of any real use at all, it will be as a clear example of the mechanics of ego-projection, self-imposed confusion and reification of ideational realities. In my estimation, Terence shows us the complete opposite of DMT's true potential. By understanding how this is so, we can begin to develop a clearer picture of what DMT is genuinely good for, and what it is not.

In order to demonstrate the above conclusions, I will carefully analyze three talks given by Terence on the subject of DMT. All three talks are available as videos on You Tube and are readily accessible for anyone to listen to on the web. The talks are, "5-MeO-DMT and nn-DMT," "Too much DMT," and "The Strangest Things Happen on DMT." I have chosen these talks for several reasons. The first is that they are available to anyone and while I am providing transcripts of the talks here in this essay, I encourage readers to listen to the talks. Tone of voice, choice of words, speech patterns, and laughter are all significant factors in evaluating what Terence shares with us. It would be even better if the talks had actual video footage so that we could also observe physical posture and body movement and gestures, but even just the audio is significantly telling.

I also wanted to include talks precisely because they are talks. While the "voice" of the author comes through in writing, spontaneous public speaking that is not from written notes, outlines, or prompts, reveals more of how someone's mind works in the moment, versus the well-thought-out and edited form of written text. In other words, to really get to know what Terence thinks of DMT, it is more insightful to talk to him or listen to him speak than to merely read anything he has written.

Lastly, I wanted to choose examples of Terence's accounts of DMT that are fairly representative. In surveying what Terence said about DMT, one quickly finds that most of his talks are fairly repetitive and he tends to touch on similar, if not identical, issues, though there are occasional inconsistencies. What this tells us is that Terence had his "rap" on DMT down fairly well, and this is what he chose to regularly share with seemingly anyone who was willing to listen. These three talks that are presented here are therefore arguably representative of his comprehensive views on the topic.

Terence lamented that there weren't enough people who were familiar with the DMT experience to really converse about it at length. In his estimation, no one had as much experience with this tryptamine as himself. He saw himself as a pioneer and as mapping new territory, so to speak. As a result, most of his public talks were one-way conversations with Terence being the sole voice of those who had gone beyond into the great mystery that was DMT.

I never met Terence. I have no idea what his level of personal use of DMT was. Nor do I know what his level of personal use of 5-MeO-DMT was, though one gets the impression that it was significantly less than of DMT. Given my own personal experience, I seriously doubt that are many people on this planet who come anywhere near my experience level with 5-MeO-DMT, and I probably have more experience with the far weaker DMT than most as well. I would be genuinely surprised if Terence had as much experience with 5-MeO as I do. And while Terence may have more experience with DMT than myself, my experience there is ample as well. I therefore feel uniquely qualified to comment on Terence's experience. Indeed, I routinely counsel people about their entheogenic experiences and help them sort out the illusions of ego from the reality of genuine being. The treatment that I will be giving Terence here is identical to what I would give to anyone who came to me with similar accounts of DMT experiences. As you read through the following, keep in mind that this is precisely the kind of assistance that I give to individuals on a daily basis.

As mentioned above, the diagnostic tool that I will be using is that of the Entheological Paradigm. As I have lectured and written a great deal on this topic, I will only present salient points here matter-of-factly. Those who are interested in more in-depth presentations should visit www.entheological-paradigm.net . The basics of the Entheological Paradigm is that all of reality can comprehensively be understood as a unified energetic system that is conscious and self-aware. The foundation of all of reality is the Energetic Unitary Being that functions according to fractal mathematics. All of reality is therefore an energetic expression of fractal patterns. This is a unitary energetic system, thereby indicating that *all* living beings are in fact *direct embodiments of the One Energy Being.*

Within the Entheological Paradigm, entheogens, or substances that "generate the experience of God within," are understood primarily as tools to open one's perception and experience of energy. This can be understood as the process of transcending the ego, which is characterized as a self-referential energetic pattern in consciousness that functions to create the perceived experience of separation between subject and object and therefore establish self-identification. However, this energetic pattern is based on the maintenance of an illusion: that of a unique, separate self. The energetic pattern of the ego is therefore *limiting*, by definition. When sufficient quantities of entheogens are ingested, shifts in one's experience of energy allow for transcendence outside of the limiting energetic confines of the ego.

Full ego transcendence is by no means the automatic result of ingestion of entheogens. Ego transcendence requires a willingness to surrender, let go, and trust completely and unconditionally. While high doses of extremely powerful entheogens such as DMT and especially 5-MeO-DMT (which is stronger than DMT by several orders of magnitude) can produce ideal experiential environments for transcending the ego, it is always a matter of choice, and it is always possible for people to choose not to let go and release. Egos that choose not to surrender and release always manage to hold on to various illusions and projections out of perceptions of self-protective fear. Energetically, this internal struggle then becomes projected out as energetic environments and visionary scenes and phenomena.

Ego transcendence is merely the beginning of genuine awakening, however. The real work is learning how to identify the products and patterns of one's ego and learning how not to let these limit oneself at any time, not just when experiencing entheogens. This then becomes a process of learning to become aware of one's energy both with and without entheogens, and thereby take responsibility for oneself as a direct embodiment of the One Energy Being. This is a long process of becoming more and more centered, aware, present, and energetically responsible. With greater personal responsibility comes greater and greater freedom, culminating in ultimate liberation from all ego-generated illusions so that one can live fully and completely in reality, right here, right now.

Given that the experience of temporary ego transcendence is just the beginning, and certainly not the end goal of entheogenic work, we can see immediately that Terence didn't even make it out the door. What we get instead are other realms with alien languages, machine elves, and self-transforming objects that amaze, confuse, and often terrify the subject of "Terence." It's all ego. 100%. In order to see how and why, let's consider carefully what Terence has to say for himself, and how he goes about saying it.

Let's take the latter issue first: how Terence communicates. For anyone not familiar with Terence's tone of voice or speaking style, you need only find any audio file of Terence and hit play to hear his distinctive, nasal voice. You can also hear, especially when he gets excited, how quickly his speech becomes fragmented. He has numerous false starts on sentences and long run-ons with endless "ands" between clauses. When he ponders questions, there are many "uhs" and "ums" mixed with "you knows" and "I means." These all reflect Terence's relationship with his subject matter, often in surprising ways.

Terence's tone of voice and nasal timbre is uniquely telling: it shows us his energetic relationship to himself and to his subject matter, the *object* he is sharing with us. The energy of his voice dramatically reveals how far Terence is from his energetic center. It tells us, immediately, *where he is coming from.*

Within the Entheological Paradigm, the human being is described as being comprised of five primary energy centers, all of which run along the central axis of the body. Three of these centers are generative of energy: they are direct energetic expressions of the Unitary Energy Being. These three are the brain (the central seat of intellectual consciousness), the heart (the central seat of conscious energetic awareness) and the sex organs (the seat of sexual energy). The two other centers are not places where energy is generated directly as in the other three, but rather process the energy of being through the physical/conscious system. Thus we also have the throat (input and output of energy and primary mechanism for personal expression through language and sound) and the stomach (regulating energy in the body in relation to the use of the throat center).

Within this system of five energy centers in the human being, the heart is the center of the total energetic system. This is the seat of "life" itself and it is the originator of the largest electro-magnetic field of the body (which far surpasses the size of the electromagnetic field produced by the brain). When one is "living from the heart," one is literally residing energetically within the center of one's being. So too when one is "speaking from the heart," one is energetically speaking from the center of one's being.

What is the energetic quality of Terence's voice? If I were to describe it, I would say that Terence appears to be speaking energetically from a point directly behind the midpoint of his brow, directly between his eyes. It is this energetic focus that gives his voice that nasal, droning quality. Physically, we can see that this energetic focus is quite distant from Terence's heart. *The very sound of his voice indicates that he is not speaking from his energetic center.* Wherever Terence is while creating his discourse, he is not in his center. Rather, he is quite clearly *in his head*, thereby indicating that he is communicating ideas; things that he thinks, rather than things he has felt or understood in the very center of his being. These are all quite clearly *ideas* for Terence, not *truths* he has experienced and felt in his heart. Keep in mind again that the electromagnetic field of your heart, the field that allows you to "feel" and "sense" your reality, is far more powerful and extends more deeply into "external" reality than that of your brain, your "thinking" organ. When the heart and brain are in energetic alignment and entrainment, what you "think" and what you "know in your heart" are in synch. However, it is quite possible for the brain to run its own energetic programs (belief systems, thought patterns, ideational constructs) independently from the heart. In other words, we are free to think anything we want, regardless of whether that is in alignment with what we can energetically experience as true with our hearts. We are also free to act on what we think or believe, regardless of the actual state of reality. This is free will. How we actualize free will, how we choose to mobilize our energy, is reflected in the energy of our bodies.

The analysis, therefore, is that Terence is talking about his ideas, but that these ideas are not in deeper alignment with the truth of his energetic center. He is disproportionately in his head; his nasal tone is an immediate expression of this fact. When one is genuinely speaking from the heart, the tone of voice tends to become deeper and more resonate, and decidedly less nasal. Patterns of speech also become more fluid, coherent, and more eloquent with far fewer false starts on sentences or words or use of fillers such as "uh" and "I mean" or "you know." This is because when one is speaking from the heart, one is simply stating the truth and does not need to "think" about what to say or how to communicate. In other words, the communication is rich, natural, and energetically expressive. You can *hear* it when someone is truly speaking from the heart (which can also clearly be distinguished from simply *impassioned* speech that can come from adherence to beliefs rather than experienced truths).

Energetically, Terence also often sounds fragmented in that he presents numerous ideas and descriptions in rapid sequence, and he also shows a lack of commitment to any specific interpretation or central point of his discourses. As a visual metaphor, one might say that he is examining and presenting all the angles, without ever looking at things from the center. Terence raises all sorts of speculations, questions, and possibilities, without ever making any definitive statements. Some might see this as a proper level of humility and ontological openness, but this isn't how Terence actually comes across. Rather, this lack of a central perspective leads him to nervous laughter and jokes about his discomfort. Energetically, his style of speech is saying, "All these ideas about my experiences are actually freaking me out a little because I can't understand how they all fit together and I seem to have a very fragmented experience of reality."

So, let's look at some of what these ideas are that are making Terence uncomfortable and lead him to over-idealize his experiences.

Our first selection is from a video entitled, "5-MeO-DMT and nn-DMT."

> *5-MeO-DMT, uh, some people like it. Uh, It's a feeling, is what it's been for me. It's this huge feeling that kind of sweeps through you and it's velvety. It's hard to describe, actually, but the main thing that I'm noticing when it's happening is I'm not hallucinating.*

Admittedly, one of the things that catches my attention most prominently in regards to Terence's attachment to DMT is how very little he has to say about 5-MeO-DMT. His preference is clearly for DMT. This is interesting for a variety of reasons. The first is that 5-MeO-DMT is so much stronger than DMT that making comparisons is difficult, if not futile. Yet this fact is not what Terence focuses on. Instead, he identifies the "main thing" as that he isn't "hallucinating" on 5-MeO-DMT. At best, he can only describe 5-MeO-DMT as "a feeling." It's huge, it sweeps through, and it's velvety. This is so vague, so overly general, that it tells us virtually nothing about the 5-MeO-DMT experience.

What is that "feeling"? I would describe it as the feeling of absolute energetic and conscious unity of all things and the certain knowledge, as experienced immediately in the energy of one's being, as your genuine self as *identical* with the Energy of All. In short, if one chooses to relax into it and open energetically to that infinite reality that certainly is beyond any kind of hallucination, then 5-MeO-DMT is the fastest and most direct route to immediately experiencing the reality of being God. Now, that's quite a "feeling," and goes so far beyond machine elves that it can render the DMT experience quaint by comparison. "Some people like it," according to Terence. It would appear that he didn't, for he has nothing more to say. "It's a feeling."

This is another clear indication that Terence was far from his energetic center. He is so removed from what he is feeling, so far more interested in hallucinating, that he doesn't even give this "feeling" a second thought. It is of no interest to him. It seems to have no value, especially when he compares it to DMT.

And of course the main thing that's happening with DMT is you're having hallucinations so intense, so 3 dimensional, so highly colored, so sculpturally defined, that it's more real than reality. And by that I mean, if you look at this room, notice how all edges are slightly feathered. There is, at all boundaries, a slight indeterminacy. But on DMT, it's hard-edged. Everything is just defined. Sometimes people say it's as though all the air had been pumped out of the room. You're seeing it with that lunar starkness and clarity, you know.

So it's the *visual* nature of DMT that Terence finds so fascinating. At lower levels, there is very little of any distinct visual quality to a 5-MeO-DMT experience and indeed, the "trip" is more something that one might feel than specifically see. However, at higher doses, 5-MeO-DMT can appear as amazingly sophisticated fractal crystalline refractions of pure white light and luminous rainbow fragments, like the most pure light shining through an unimaginably complex prism. Yet DMT still seems to have a more distinct visual nature to it than 5-MeO-DMT, so to some extent, here Terence is being reasonably accurate. By comparison, DMT is more an infinite spectrum of colors and geometry and patterns that can be visually hyper-distinct and appear in mind-boggling detail.

Notice, however, that Terence doesn't describe the *feeling*, and when he does make an attempt to characterize this visual quality, he dovetails into an odd statement about air being pumped out of a room and then tops it off with "lunar starkness and clarity, followed by a "you know." Chances are, we don't, actually, know what Terence means by that. Does he?

In terms of the energetic *feeling* made accessible by 5-MeO-DMT versus DMT, the *feeling* of 5-MeO-DMT is far stronger. Despite the more intense visual nature of DMT, the feeling, by comparison, is extremely mild. The energetic opening (and opportunity to deeply transcend the ego) afforded by 5-MeO-DMT is much, much stronger than DMT. In fact, with DMT, one might not "feel" anything, and instead, get almost entirely fixated on what one is *seeing*, the *objects* of experience, rather than the experience itself.

Let's see what Terence goes on to mention:

And unimaginable objects. Objects off the art scale.

> *And entities. DMT is the only one of these psychedelics where I have seen the entities. On psilocybin, it speaks. And it's audio. On DMT, it's, it's uh, you see these things. And, uh, I don't know whether it's my personal mythology . . .*

So not only objects, but even more significantly, *entities*. Terence is impressed with DMT not only for it's hyper-real and super-detailed objects, but also for the entities that he encounters. Yet he immediately expresses his confusion about these beings. What are they? His "personal mythology"? And even if they are, what are they doing here, in the DMT experience? Why is he *seeing* them?

Terence has no idea. This phenomenon is literally boggling his mind. As much as he is trying, he can't wrap his head "around" it, despite all the energy he's concentrating directly behind the bridge of his nose.

> *For me, DMT is the center of the mystery. I fear it. I love it. I thank God for it. Uh, I wonder if I'll ever understand it. It takes a huge mustering of courage on my part to do it, because I . . . it's just so . . . I mean, we talk talk talk talk talk, change transformation, other dimensions . . . this is not talk, when you do that. I mean, you just do not know the parameters. I feel like I know more of what could happen to me if I'm in the Amazon jungle than I know what could happen to me when I'm in that place. And after many, many DMT trips, I've finally been able to paint a picture for myself of what is happening in there.*

This is an extremely telling passage for Terence. He openly admits his fear, his lack of understanding, his struggle with DMT. He even seems to question why he's so attracted to it at all, given the unimaginable strangeness it has presented to him. Yet he is so perplexed and fascinated by his experiences that they have become the "center of the mystery" for Terence. They are the ultimate puzzle. And it terrifies him. It requires "a huge mustering of courage" to embark on such a journey and to contemplate such an enigmatic object. So at best, he's painted a picture for himself. He has *constructed an idealized representation*, a "painting," of what he *thinks* is "happening *in there*."

Notice Terence's use of language, especially when taken into consideration in the context of the energy of his being while speaking this. I've already described Terence as being distant from his energetic center as he appears to be energetically speaking from a point centered between his eyes. He claims that what he is telling us is the "center of the mystery," yet his energy does not correlate with this linguistic claim. The energy that underlies the words is saying, "I'm presenting you with an idealized visual representation," but it is not *from the center*. Indeed, Terence even tells us as much when he describes his account as a "picture," clearly referencing the idealized visual nature of his understanding that rests far from the center of his heart. This is clearly *not* the *center of the mystery*.

> *And what happens for me – and I don't know anybody who's done it as much as I have – I wish people did it more and talked more about it, because boy, if there is a landscape where we need more consensus, this is it. I have been present when people did it, and they come back babbling about the same thing that I think I have encountered. I mean, they come back, and one woman said, "It was a carnival. It was a carnival. It was an extra-terrestrial midway." Somebody else came back and said, "There were gnomes. There were elves." And, yeah. This is getting close to it.*

Terence laments that he is one of the few that have been to the center of the mystery and come back to give any reports about it, presenting himself as a lone explorer into the unknown realms. He feels himself to be somewhat affirmed by others, who appear to speak his language about the objects and contents of the experience, but still, it's only "close." He's looking for universals, but they aren't easily forthcoming. Are gnomes the same as elves the same as alien carnival as machine elf? How could one possibly know?

How much influence is Terence having over others? I don't just mean a psychological influence, which is certainly present as Terence spoke about his experiences openly, thereby potentially influencing anyone tripping with him. But even more profoundly, from the perspective of the Entheological Paradigm, all of reality is understood as a singular energetic system. In practical terms, what this means is that despite appearances, there is really only one being, and that one being is all things. As such, the one being engages in game playing between contrived subjects and perceived objects. Terence, as a manifestation of the one being, is providing himself with self-validating experiences in the form of others who tell him enough to convince himself of the reality of the game he is playing. Generally speaking, we draw to ourselves those who will validate our ego-generated narratives of who we think we are and what we think is occurring within our lives. It is a game, however, and those with illusory personal narratives can always find others to play along.

> *What happens to me when I do it is, um . . . I'm conveyed – there's a period, an initial period of a kind of hysteria and*

confusion. It's almost as though time speeds up, even before you take the first hit. Many people say, just before you do DMT, there's this funny kind of impression in the room, almost as though there's a backwash from the event about to happen. You're caught in the psychic field of this event, and everything is moving faster and faster – this is like the q phenomenon - and then you take the hit, and it's building up in your body, and your heart is pounding, and everything and then you break through to this place.

Despite Terence's propensity to immediately jump to time-backwash speculative metaphysics, given that he describes the onset of the DMT experience as one of hysteria and confusion, it's not difficult to imagine that he is merely experiencing anxiety in anticipation of the big event. While confusion is not uncommon among novice users of any psychedelic, it is somewhat surprising that with all of Terence's professed use of DMT, he never got beyond the feelings of hysteria and confusion. Notice that this is the first time that he attempts to describe the *feeling* of DMT, though he doesn't describe the feeling directly – only his emotional and psychological reaction: hysteria and confusion. Notice also that he identifies from the beginning with the concept that DMT takes you to a *place*, somewhere that you must "break through" into, and therefore is distinctly characterized as *other* or *not here*. Wherever DMT seems to take Terence, in his mind, it is definitely not here. This is a clear indication that Terence is dealing with ego projections. When one is centered, present, relaxed, trusting, and open, no medicine, no matter how potentially powerful, will take you anywhere but *right here, right now*. Anything less than that is an energetic reaction of the ego resisting the energy of being completely centered and present.

And what it's like is, the first impression is of a loud, well the first impression is of the sound of cellophane being crumpled – that crackling sound as if someone had just taken a bread wrapper – (audience laughs) – yeah – (more laughter), crackle that cellophane for us! (T laughs with audience) – That's it! (more laughter, louder) More of that! (more loud laughter – audience member calls out, "Are we there yet?")

Would that it were so easy! A friend of mine says, "That's the sound of the radio-entelechy of your soul tearing out of the organic envelope" (audience laughs more and T joins in with a nervous laugh). Which is what it sounds like. It sounds like your body has just been wadded up and thrown into a corner and now you're a radio signal approximately 4 light seconds in diameter spreading out through an alien universe.

Here we see that Terence is willing to quickly jump from an occasionally experienced phenomenon, that of hearing cellophane crinkling, to metaphysical speculations about the relationship between "body" and "soul." The first fact that deserves comment here is that hearing a sound that resembles cellophane crinkling is a somewhat common, yet nowhere near universal, feature of DMT ingestion. Terence speaks of this phenomenon as though it is a constant, so perhaps this occurred for Terence every time he smoked DMT and he made the incorrect assumption that this is true for everyone. It definitely isn't, though it does show up enough to make it an interesting phenomenon. If we wanted to be scientific about it, we would see if there were any correlation between the perception of the sound and the subsequent quality of the DMT experience. However, Terence is not being scientific here. He's speculating.

Terence's speculation is largely nonsensical. He knows it too. His nervous laugh communicates as much. The energy of his laugh seems to say, "This is totally absurd, but I believe it anyway!" There is no sound of heartfelt confidence – just uncomfortable questions.

Terence again tips his hand and demonstrates the deep level of disassociation that DMT causes him. He completely disassociates from his body, and with it, consensual reality, and envisions his "soul," (a concept that is dismissed within the Entheological Paradigm as a clear product of ego projection) as leaving this world for an *alien* universe. Terence finds DMT to be *alienating* from reality.

And the next impression is of a cheer. It's, "Hurrah! Welcome! Welcome!" And it's them, and they're waiting. And they can hardly wait. There's a moment where there not on me - just a moment. And then they say, "You're here! We're glad to see you. Why did you stay away so long?" and then they come toward me.

Now we have reached the true crux of the experience for Terence: the beings! He opened his talk by saying that DMT was more significant for him than 5-MeO-DMT because the former makes him hallucinate whereas the latter doesn't. But even more significant than this, Terence is captivated by DMT as it is the only psychedelic he's used that has allowed him to experience "beings," and he is clearly deeply fascinated by this. *This* is what makes DMT the center of the mystery for Terence.

Is it possible to make sense of what's going on here?

> *And the main thing for me in the DMT thing is to struggle not to go into shock of wonder, basically. I mean, because there is a tendency, a strong tendency, and for the first few trips, I couldn't conquer it, I was just, I was a victim of it, and I would go into this (presumably makes a face of wonder or astonishment – audience laughs). You know and I would say, "Heart, heart OK. Breathing, breathing OK." But I'm looking, and I can't believe my eyes, because I'm in some kind of domed place. And the impression, don't ask my why, but the impression is of being underground, even though it's a huge vaulted space, and highly colored. And then . . . but what is of course riveting my attention is these beings. They're small, and they're like, and I've described them as machine elves – they seem partially machine-like and partially elf-like.*

Terence is clearly awed by his experience of the so-called "machine elves." His descriptions of his awe are very telling – shock and wonder that he couldn't "conquer." DMT does give rise to tremendous feelings of awe and wonder, so there's nothing that strange or unusual for Terence to be making such claims. However, given that Terence describes his experiences rather uniformly, along with his claims of having taken more DMT than anyone he's ever come across, we do have an interesting situation here. I would diagnose him as being stuck. Based on his descriptions, we're given the impression that *every time* Terence takes DMT, he is awed and shocked at *fundamentally the same thing, time and time again*. Terence has *nothing more* to share about DMT. It's all machine elves and self-transforming jeweled objects. There's no movement. There are no breakthroughs. There are no realizations. There is no recognition of the self. Terence is stuck. It's machine elves, every time, and it awes him.

The productive use of any entheogen will move, change, and progress. For Terence to begin and end with machine elves shows that he has not used his DMT experiences to come to any greater understanding or acceptance of himself. He fixated on his ideas of the machine elves and never got beyond them. He reified them into a permanent feature of his experience.

> *(audience member asks unintelligible question)*

> *No, they are not so mundane as that – they don't have a fixed body outline. And in fact, that's one of the things going on in*

this space that's so baffling. They come toward you, they're singing in this alien language, which you somehow understand. It cannot be translated into English, but you understand it in that moment. And what they are doing is, they're using their voices to produce objects, so song becomes thing.

And there are dozens of these things, and they're coming closer and closer and the songs they sing condense into objects, and the objects themselves can sing, and these things come and they're saying, "Look, look" and they're holding this stuff out to you, and you look at it, and you're fighting wonder because your entire being is caught up in "This can't be happening!" and yet they're saying, you know, "Just look!"

And what these things are, are devices, toys, works of art, objects . . . But whatever they are, they are amazing. And you look into it, and you can't, and they seem to be shifting, even though they're made of metal and glass and gems and pulsating . . . everything is migrating and shifting and changing and they say, "Look at this one," and it's the most astonishing thing you've ever seen, and you look at it, and they say, "Look at this one! Look at this one!" And they're piling up and these things are coming toward you and then they jump through you – they can pass through your body, and they're running around chirping and singing and making these objects and what they're doing is, what they're saying is, "Do what we are doing. Do what we are doing," and you say, uh . . . "I just want to go back to New York!" (audience laughs and Terence joins in with a nervous laugh of his own)

In the above we have the grand crescendo of Terence's DMT experiences. Virtually every account he gives of DMT centers around the supposed production of objects through the use of song, or what Terence otherwise describes as "alien language." Terence seems to feel that this is a monumental discovery and at some level, a metaphysical truth about reality: the world is made of language. These bizarre experiences with the machine elves seem to confirm this view – indeed, elsewhere Terence challenges those who don't believe that reality is made out of language to take DMT and then see what they think of the proposition.

This view only makes sense if you believe in magic, which Terence clearly does. In fact, this belief is central to Terence's entire relationship to psychedelics and is foundational to virtually everything he has said about psychedelics. In answer to Terence's rhetorical question of whether his

DMT experiences were products of his "personal mythology," is an emphatic, "Yes, obviously."

One need only dig a little into Terence's history to see how this personal mythology has played out for Terence. In his written work, such as *True Hallucinations*, Terence writes of how he began his psychedelic quest by venturing into the South American jungle in search of the "violet psychofluid of translinguistic matter" that is reportedly excreted by ayahuasca-using shamans in the Amazon. In other words, Terence is specifically looking for the connections between language, reality, and psychedelics. He's searching for something *very particular*. He's not looking for "truth" or "reality," and certainly not looking for "himself." He's looking for violet psychofluid of translinguistic matter. He has his sights set on a very particular object that dovetails perfectly into his philosophical speculations that reality is somehow made out of language.

Apparently, Terence found "it" in his construction of the machine elves, their alien realm, and their strange behavior of creating objects out of sound. However, upon making this "discovery," Terence is nothing but confused and dumbfounded. He can make no sense of this whatsoever. Jokingly, he remarks that he just wants to go home. It's just too strange, too nonsensical, too enigmatic. It all seems to have no applicability, unless one thinks magically, like Terence. In the end, Terence concluded that this strange ability to manifest objects through sound and language is connected to his speculations on 2012. Elsewhere, he writes that in 2012 we'll be able to climb into UFO's that we speak or sing into existence, just like the machine elves, and we'll fly off to join the great cosmic community. Terence clearly believes in magic.

Quite interestingly, and also quite unscientifically, Terence appears to have never taken the next step in his machine elf reveries: actually attempting to do as they are instructing him. I have not found a single reference to Terence taking the machine elves' advice or instruction. He repeatedly tells us that the machine elves are instructing him to "not be amazed" and "just do it," meaning to sing an object into existence. Yet at virtually every recounting of his DMT experiences, he tells us that this he is dumbfound by this command. Odd, isn't it, that he never attempts the one thing they tell him to do?

What would it mean for Terence to try to sing something into existence and why are the elves telling him this? The answer is, I think, not at all what Terence might imagine. With the perspective that the machine elves are projections of Terence's ego, and therefore actually versions of himself, the command to sing speaks volumes. I've already shown how drastically disassociated Terence is from his body in his DMT experiences. He is completely in a "mental" space that is entirely disconnected from simply being here, now. He struggles intellectually with what he encounters in this mental space. He's trying to make sense of it. However, the elves urge Terence not to try and make sense of it. They simply urge him to "do what we do" and "don't be amazed."

However, for Terence to actually try to do what the machine elves are supposedly doing would require Terence to *feel his body, be present with himself and stop obsessing with the machine elves.* The man would have to actually attempt to sing. He would have to mobilize energy in his body and consciously direct it with his voice and intentions. Yet Terence is convinced that he's a disembodied soul in an alien universe and his body is wadded up in a ball, discarded in the corner of the room. He is completely disassociated from the genuine reality of his being. Singing, then, would seem to be an impossible feat. He's too busy trying to understand to even contemplate being in his body and being present.

Terence is stuck in his ideas, beliefs, and ego-generated mythology about the nature of reality. The elves, ironically, are actually giving Terence advice for "getting back to reality," despite the appearance of things being otherwise. As versions of himself, they are telling Terence: Don't be amazed! Just try singing and see how *your experience of reality shifts and changes with the mobilization of your energy.* The elves are attempting to get Terence energetically and consciously back in his body and out of the bizarre mental space he's created for himself and subsequently become obsessively attached to. In a sense, they're saying, "Stop your obsessive thinking and try feeling." Terence, however, didn't get the message. After all, he just wants to go home.

Our next selection comes from a clip entitled "The Strangest Things Happen on DMT." Here, Terence reiterates many of the ideas given above, as well as adds an archetypal interpretation of the circus to the DMT experience. As with the above account, what we again find, despite claims to the counter, is that the experiences are entirely reflective of Terence and his own energy rather than revealing any kinds of secrets about the universe – at least, not in the way that he assumes.

> *The strangest things happen on DMT – the most intense – and you can remember them. DMT is not like a psychedelic drug in the sense that you're getting into the contents of your hopes, memories, fears and dreams – It's much more like a parallel continuum. It's more as though, uh, you've broken through to some alien data space.*

Once again we can immediately see that Terence wants to distinguish the DMT experience as characterized by a pervasive sense of *otherness.* Here, he even goes so far as to proclaim DMT's supposed otherness from other psychedelics, which he identifies as providing access to one's "personal content." I would have to thoroughly disagree, and I think that the analysis given above adequately proves that, as will the analyses provided below. The difference is largely one of magnitude and intensity, but not necessarily in kind. Being a tryptamine, and also being the active ingredient in ayahuasca, DMT is very similar to psilocybin mushrooms and the ayahuasca experience. The duration is much shorter and the intensity can be many, many times greater, as can be the visual quality of the experience, but none of these are entirely dissimilar from each other. Even 5-MeO-DMT is experientially of a similar nature. In fact, *all* entheogenic medicines are the same in the sense that they open up one's ability to perceive and experience energy. They do this in different ways and at different levels of intensity (with 5-MeO-DMT being of the greatest intensity, by far), but in that sense they are all "the same." The difference is in degree. There are other significant differences, but in the end, energy is energy and you either feel it and perceive it or you don't.

Take music, for example. You can hear (perceive the energy of) a piece of music in a multitude of ways depending on your state of mind, your emotional state, your personal associations with the music, and on and on. The music is the same. The way you experience it differs. Medicines work in a similar fashion in that they all open you to energy, but in somewhat different ways and capacities.

Yet Terence insists that DMT is different in that he does not see it as reflecting personal perceptions, like other medicines, and in fact sends you to an alien realm. The greatest difference here is in Terence's estimation, not necessarily the medicines themselves. Certainly there are plenty of shamans out there who would equally claim that ayahuasca and mushrooms have the capacity to take one into "another realm," which Terence is here seemingly willing to dismiss as personal projection, a point with which I'd gladly agree. But not DMT. DMT is special, according to Terence. This is where Terence and I differ.

> *One of the most puzzling things about DMT is that it doesn't affect your mind, you know. It simply replaces the world, 100% with something completely unexpected. But your relationship to that unexpected thing is not one of exaggerated fear, or exaggerated acceptance, as in "Oh great, the world has just been replaced by elf machinery!" Your reaction is exactly what it would be if it happened to you without DMT – you're appalled! You say, "What happened?" Because you don't feel your mind moving. You just see that the world has been replaced*

*by something that you could not have even conceived of or
imagined before.*

Terence is here extrapolating far beyond the available data to
entirely unsupported conclusions, which he simply presents as universal
fact. *His* experiences with DMT seem to 100% replace the world, and
certainly this seems to be true of enough of other peoples' experiences to
give it some validity. But then, how does one account for the fact that it is
quite possible for people to consume even very large doses of DMT
without having a "world replacing" experience? Again, I point out that
individuals who are energetically centered and present can consume large
quantities of entheogens with little to virtually no perceptual distortion or
change at all. In fact, the more present, centered, and focused one gets,
while simultaneously relaxing, trusting, and completely letting go, the more
profoundly "normal" any entheogenic experience becomes. But Terence is
anything but centered, focused, relaxed, present, and trusting. In fact,
everything indicates that he is, energetically, of the exact opposite state.
Given his energetic state, *his* reactions to DMT are *entirely expected.* They
are not "normal," in the sense that these are the reactions of a severely
energetically wound up being. Those who are more relaxed, trusting,
present, and able to let go of their ideational realities have very different
experiences from Terence, and in my estimation, for the better.

Part of the difficulty here is the experience of realities that "you
could not have conceived of or imagined before," and this is certainly an
apt description for the visions afforded by tryptamines. However, we have
confusions of subject, object, and ultimate identity here. From the ego's
perspective, yes, all these "realms" and their unimaginable contents do
seem "unimaginable" and appear unrelated to the self. Yet, the question
then becomes: what actually is the self? Is the self what the ego thinks it is,
or is it something else entirely? Who, actually, is the author of all this
visionary content? Is it "me," or something "other."

The "natural" reaction on the part of most egos is to assume, given
the grandeur of the experience, that some "other" is involved in its
production. Initial impressions can be radically deceiving, however, and
those initial impressions can get energetically stuck if one attempts to wrap
too much ideational structure around the impressions. For advanced
practitioners, it becomes increasingly apparent and undeniable that *all*
contents of entheogenic experiences are projections of the self. It just
becomes obvious, though admittedly, this is only for those who reach a
deep level of self-acceptance and responsibility. However, at that level, it
becomes immediately clear that one's own thoughts, emotions, and
reactions have a direct effect on the contents of visionary experience – even

the seemingly most radical, alien, and otherworldly. Once you see through the veil of self-produced illusion, the truth becomes undeniable. It is you. It's been you all along. You just didn't know how to recognize yourself.

Within the Entheological Paradigm, visionary states of consciousness are characterized as experiences of the Divine Imagination. The fundamental building blocks of experience within the Divine Imagination are fractal and geometric patterns of energy, which, indeed, are the energetic blueprints for all of reality. Within this perceptual energetic space, the energy of egoic consciousness bounces off the fundamental matrix of energy, so to speak, and creates images related to the individual's consciousness. The simplest way to put it is that when gazing into the Divine Imagination, one is looking into a mirror that expresses the fullness of one's energetic being. Visions are a form of communication from the self to the self. Ego's however, get very confused about what is going on in this process as they perceive the contents of consciousness as being distinct from the subject experiencing it. This is a fundamental mis-perception and is grounded in energetic illusion rather than energetic truth. It is a product of the ego. Individuals who are not confused and who are centered don't have visions in the Divine Imagination as they are able to perceive themselves as they actually are: energy. Confused egos have visions. Confused egos see "content."

To be clear, if Terence were centered and present, his DMT experiences wouldn't take him anywhere but *right here, right now*. The fact that they don't is a clear reflection of the imbalances in his personal energy.

And these entities, these things that look like self-dribbling jeweled basket balls – something that the NBA might take an interest in – you see them. They present themselves to you. They use language to condense visible objects out of the air.

Now, I don't know why they're doing that. Perhaps at one level I assume they're trying to teach you how to do that. On another level they seem to be giving a demonstration that reality is made out of language. They're saying, "Hey, you don't believe reality is made out of language? Here, I'll make you one." And then blibbledy bliddledy blip, and there they hand you one and it's to be passed around with slack jawed amazement among the human beings. This technology that they possess of these objects made out of gold and emeralds and chalcedony and agate, that are morphing themselves, even as you look at them – I mean, this is a technological dream come true – the lapis as elf excrescence or something like that - and why they're there – I don't know.

Did Terence ever ponder how this might be a reflection of himself? Does he not realize that he, himself, is making exotic "objects" out of language by putting thoughts into the minds of others of machine elves and self-dribbling basketballs and reality made out of language? Isn't this a perfect metaphor for *exactly what Terence is himself doing?*

> *Many, many questions. Where are they when you're not stoned? Do they have an autonomous existence somewhere? Do they spring into existence a micro-second before you get there? Are they rooted in the dynamics of your psyche, or are they no more rooted in the dynamics of your psyche than the world trade center? It's not clear.*

I've already provided the answer to these questions: Terence, they are all a reflection of yourself, even if you are unable to accept the reality of this. You are the machine elves and the self-dribbling basketballs. They exist only when you smoke DMT and shift your perception to the Divine Imagination as they are merely reflections of yourself. And now that you've become attached to them, you are using them to play games with yourself, providing yourself with data for your pet theories about the nature of reality that, when considered carefully, don't actually make sense, which is why you always find this game so confounding and confusing: a riddle with no solution, an endless puzzle to ponder. This, Terence, is a self-referential mobius strip of reality of your own creation. To transcend it, you must take responsibility for it and learn to recognize yourself.

Of course, now that you've shared these experiences with the world, you've inspired so many others to go out in search of machine elves. And you know what? They've seen them too! Why? Because the illusions of your ego spoke to the illusions of their egos, and they too find themselves reflected back to themselves in the form of machine elves and self-dribbling basketballs. Congratulations, Terence! Your words have created new objects in hyperspace! You did it! You can relax and trust and let go now. Mission accomplished!

> *I think I mentioned at some point, just briefly, that the archetype of DMT is the circus. These things are clowns, at one level. They're clowns. When you think of the circus, it's a very complex archetype. The circus is for children. It's a delight. You take a child to the circus that there's three rings and absurd clown antics going on, but then you lift your eyes up to the top of the tent and there the lady in the tiny spangled costume is hanging by her*

teeth and working without a net. It's about eros and death. My first awareness of eros was being 3 or 4 and these women in these tiny costumes spinning around realizing, you know, if she falls, she dies. And then away from the center ring and all this action there are the sideshows: the goat faced boy, the thing in the bottle, the Siamese twins and fuzzy Charlie . . . all of that is also very DMT-like. It really is the archetype of the circus.

I can remember when I was a kid in this small town in Colorado, every 4ᵗʰ of July the carnival would come to town for a week and set up and we anticipated it all year. But as soon as they were there, we couldn't play outside after 9 at night because the carny people are different, we were told. And their means of support, sexual proclivities and choice of intoxicants might have run counter to this mid-western Catholic mining town I was in. So there's this sense the disruption, the danger, the drama, the interest, the fun, and then they go away, and life is as if they had never been there at all. And that's what DMT is like.

And the mobius strip takes another turn. Terence just can't see himself, despite the fact that he references himself and his childhood experiences. He claims that the circus is the "archetype" of DMT, and then goes on to claim that this is so because it reminds him of his childhood experiences at the circus. Hello! Self to Terence! Pay attention!

I will emphatically state that the "circus" is *not* in any way the "archetype" of DMT. This is *Terence's*, and perhaps those whom he associates with, archetype of DMT. Given that the DMT experience is one of the infinite energetic nature of the self, it can be anything. Granted, it is very colorful, wildly entertaining, extraordinarily fun and exhilarating, so maybe it's like a circus in that sense – though perhaps Burning Man would be a more apt imagistic metaphor. But exhilaration and pretty lights do not necessarily Burning Man, or a circus, make. DMT is its own experience and is not reflective of any other archetype, other than possibly all archetypes.

For Terence, the circus represents danger, sexuality, liminality, otherness, and suspension of ordinary social interactions and realities. It is exotic and thrilling for him. It's entertainment, but with an edge. It's also a temporary reality and ephemeral. It's completely disconnected from ordinary life. It represents all that is not usually *here, now.* For a small child in a rural Catholic community, the circus is pure alien thrill and an escape from mundane reality, but only for a little while, and most of the normal responsibilities of life and being have nothing to do with the liminal state of the circus.

The fact that this is the archetype for DMT for Terence tells us volumes about how he approached and appreciated his DMT experiences. Just like the circus, they were temporary diversions into liminality, completely disconnected from the ordinary world and ordinary life. Completely and thrillingly *other*.

This represents a profound internal dichotomy within Terence and his energetic being. He is being dualistic to the extreme. Again, centered and present individuals who use entheogenic experiences to bring themselves into the clarity of being precisely where and who they are find DMT to be *profoundly unitary*. In other words, they don't experience DMT as being dualistic at all. Rather, the energetic unity of all of reality is immediately perceived and experienced at all levels of one's energetic being. There is *nothing* even remotely *other* about such experiences. In fact, in unitary states of consciousness, perception of *otherness* is actually impossible (if it were possible, it wouldn't be unitary consciousness).

Another way of putting this is to say that Terence's choice of archetypes is a reflection of his lack of mystical, unitary perception. *Terence did not experience the oneness of all things. He experienced profound separation and alienation.*

> *I mean, it's a secret of such magnitude that it's inconceivable how it has ever been kept. In a world where information was fairly weighted, we would spend as much time talking a bout DMT as we do about, I don't know, the West Bank or something. And as you see from studying our newspapers, DMT is rarely, if ever, mentioned. I mean, never would be a good rule of thumb.*

Times are changing and this is not anywhere near as true now as it was when Terence spoke these words. Part of that discussion about DMT needs to be on the supposed reality of what is encountered within the DMT experience. This is precisely what is taking place here in this essay. While Terence might have been shocked by my conclusions or taken personal offence at them (egos often have a difficult time hearing the truth), honestly assessing his testimony in fact is more respectful than blind acceptance. At least I'm taking Terence seriously. If DMT is going to part of the public discourse, as it is increasingly becoming, informed perspectives become all the more vital.

> *The Western mind is very queasy around these experiences that cast into doubt their illusions about how reality is put together. When you get to DMT, you have hit the main vein. I mean, I hold it in reserve as the ultimate convincer. I mean, there are these people*

running around who say, "You people are into drugs – give me a branch whiskey and a little TV – I think you're deluding yourselves." "Do you? Well do you have 5 minutes to invest in this cheerful proposition, my friend, because have I got news for you!"

I would definitely agree with the opening statement above, and also add that people in general are wary of experiences that challenge their beliefs. Beliefs are what egos are made of, in many respects. Most egos aren't all that willing to let themselves dissolve into the infinite expanse of their genuine natures when it means letting go of everything they've ever thought or believed. Intellectuals can be just as bad as religious fundamentalists, though, for ideas can be just as difficult to transcend as beliefs.

The proposed use of DMT to replace one set of beliefs with another is a waste of time and energy. All beliefs are limiting energetic constructs and while some sets of beliefs are more realistic than others, they are all still beliefs. Fortunately, entheogens such as DMT, and especially 5-MeO-DMT, can assist in the transcendence of all beliefs and direct perception and experience of the infinite, unified energetic nature of reality, right here, right now. This is not what Terence is using DMT to do, however, and he is clearly caught in his belief structures and ideational realities that he is creating for himself. He could transcend all of this, if he would only choose to. Somewhat disappointingly, Terence rather sees DMT as a tool to convince someone of the reality of an illusionary belief system. How is this different from religious indoctrination?

Our final selection is entitled "Too Much DMT," and quite fittingly, somewhat addresses the above question.

Right in the middle of this trip, this woman came back to the house . . . and started beating on my door furiously. Now being a double Scorpio and secretive anyway, I just about had a heart attack and jumped off the bed right off this DMT flash. I jumped up and landed on my feet in the middle of this room. And something about moving so suddenly had shattered the distinction between the two continuums and I carried it all with me so that the room was then filled with elves. They were hanging off my arms and spinning me around and there was this geometric object in the room that was spinning and clicking. And every time it would click, it would hurl a plastic chip across the room that had a letter in an alien language written on it. And these elves were screaming and bouncing off the walls. This machine was spinning in the air. The chips are ricocheting off the walls, and I was trying to deal with Rosemary in the middle of this.

And you know, it was a too-muchness. It was a case of seeing too deeply into it. And if you have too many of those kinds of trips, then you become reluctant. This is why I'm very cautious with it. The notion of having enough chutzpa or will or something to want to try use this stuff – I can hardly imagine using it – I mean, every time I encounter it, my wish is not to be destroyed by it. And the idea of using it for anything just seems like blasphemy, you know – and it probably is blasphemy – probably a good way to get cut down to size.

Too much, indeed. The most interesting way to view this account of too-muchness is to appreciate the fullness of the perspective provided by the Entheological Paradigm. Keep in mind, not only is Terence everything that he experiences on DMT, but he is also everything that he experiences without DMT. There is only One Being, after all, and that being is everything, including Terence and his DMT trips. So, from that perspective, what is going on here?

First of all, we see Terence firmly identifying with his ego in recounting this story. He rationalizes that his reaction to having his door pounded on furiously by a woman immediately after launching into a DMT trip was due not only to being "secretive," but also a "double Scorpio." Astrology is an ego's dream: finding personal, egoic meaning in the movement of stars and planets and providing rationales for personal patterns of behavior. It's ego story telling at its finest. Realistically, Terence could just say that anyone pounding on anyone's door immediately after ingesting DMT would probably be disquieting. He doesn't say that, however. He wraps a couple layers of ego around a simple statement.

From the perspective of the Entheological Paradigm, understand that the being that is Terence is also the disruptive woman, Rosemary, as well. In this case, it seems as though the One Being decided that it was time to shake Terence up and force him to reconsider this energetic, dualistic divide he had created between "DMT Space" and "normal" reality. The pounding on the door forced Terence to come out of his psychedelic head space of alien realms and deal with the fact that he's actually a person in a body in a room tripping DMT and not a "radio entelechy of the soul" parading about in an alien universe. The *truth* is that Terence is actually right here, right now, and the woman pounding on the door it about to prove it.

However, Terence's attachment to his fantasy projections are literally gambling with his life and wellbeing. He's so attached that the screaming, bounding machine elves are hanging off him, clinging to him (and by mirror reflection, he to them). And in the middle of it all is some strange machine, spitting out alien poker chips randomly about the room while Terence tries to deal with the irate woman.

Too much, indeed. And all that Terence can say about this event is that the *sudden movement* caused his distinction between the "two continuums" to collapse, thereby bringing it all back with him into normal reality. Terence's dualism shines through yet again. His mind space is different from his body space. They are two different continuums. Terence does not experience himself as an integrated person. He is not present in his being. And this experience is a way for Terence to show himself this truth through the context of the woman and the elves jumping about the room and the poker chips. It was a lesson. A harsh one. If embraced, it could lead him to the next step in the process of recognition of the self and letting go of false beliefs.

It seems to have scared Terence. Once his dualistic distinctions got shaken up, he seems to have become less cavalier about DMT. He directly states that he fears that the DMT experience will destroy him. Ironically, this is precisely the kind of experience his ego needs to go through. The surprise would be that once he fully surrendered to the process of being destroyed, he'd find himself present and liberated. It's only a temporary transcendence of the ego, after all, not "the end." In fact, it's just the beginning.

So shaken by this experience was he that Terence goes on to claim that using DMT for anything is blasphemous. Indeed, it is terrifying to challenge one's belief systems. Challenging beliefs is the very definition of blasphemous, and it is the fear and terror that this causes the ego that has led religions to react so strongly to the blasphemous. False identities built on belief in illusions don't want to hear the truth of what they are. In that sense, use of DMT to transcend beliefs is blasphemous, in the best possible way.

When used consciously, entheogens hold the radical potential to be the ultimate tools in self-awakening and human liberation. They can bring us to direct and immediate experience of the true energetic nature of reality and ourselves as embodiments of the Unitary Energy. One has to choose to let go, however, of all beliefs and all ideas produced by the ego. These are blocks and they only serve to get in the way between ourselves and genuine reality.

Using DMT to affirm beliefs is just delusional, in the worst way. We are not what we think we are. We are not what any of our belief systems have taught. Beliefs just get in the way and project out as all kinds of illusions and fictions to which we react exactly as our egos have trained themselves to react. Terence is a great example of this truth and his DMT experiences clearly show this ego mechanism at work in the Divine Imagination. It's too late for Terence to go beyond his illusions of the machine elves. Fortunately, it's not too late for the rest of us.

DMT.

It's an interactive mirror.

Enjoy the show.

But don't be fooled by the clowns. It's just an act, after all.

;-)

Energy, Ego, and Entheogens:
The Reality of Human Liberation from Illusion

Recently, I published an article entitled "Terence on DMT," where I strongly critiqued Terence McKenna for his popular lectures on DMT. The gist of the article was that what Terence described as the "DMT experience" should more properly be described as "Terence's DMT experience" as I showed that the majority of what he had to say on the subject, at least at the popular/public level, was generated by his ego and therefore is best understood as personal projection. To illustrate these conclusions, I applied what I have come to call the "Entheological Paradigm" to Terence's public talks, as available on Youtube videos.

The article generated a great deal of resistance and backlash, as expected, as well as some serious questions. Issuing a no-holds-barred critique of a well-loved and extremely popular public figure isn't exactly a way to win friends, but it is effective for provoking people. My main aim was to demonstrate that entheogenic experiences are not mysterious and can be fully explained and understood from a naturalistic perspective that does not require belief in any "other realms" or "other beings." When entheogenic experiences are properly understood for what they are – energetic experiences that exhibit a dynamic relationship between the ego and universal self – the most bizarre experiences can easily be identified as expressions and constructs of the grasping ego. Another aim was to raise the issue of human liberation from self-generated illusion and the suffering that results from such illusions. The purpose of this essay here is to follow up on this particular idea with a clear analysis of the energetic nature of entheogens and their relationship to the energy mobilized and structured by the ego.

The Entheological Paradigm:

I will begin by mentioning that I have made the Entheological Paradigm available to the public as lectures on my podcast, "The Entheogenic Evolution," in my book, *Being Human: An Entheological Guide to God, Evolution, and the Fractal Energetic Nature of Reality,* as videos on Youtube, as a website, www.entheological-paradigm.net, and as public lectures at events like Burning Man. In my book, *Being Human,* I write, on page 57, "A common effect of working with entheogens is attachment to story. People see visions or encounter other 'beings' and then proceed to weave fantastic stories around their experiences. Terence McKenna and the infamous machine elves are an excellent case in point."

I have yet to receive a single complaint from a reader of *Being Human* for that passage and the sentences that follow. My recent article was simply the full analysis of the reality of that claim. Therefore, for those who have followed my work, this was nothing new, nor, unexpected. However, for many readers, I'm sure that this was their first exposure to the Entheological Paradigm (and my provocative communication style). My suggestion for all interested readers is to take a look at *Being Human* and see what you think. At the least, it is my hope that this article will help generate deeper understanding of the Entheological Paradigm and why it is significant for understanding not only entheogenic experiences, but reality as a whole, including one's understanding of the genuine nature of the self.

The Entheological Paradigm is not a system of beliefs, metaphysics, or spirituality. As the name suggests, it is a descriptive model of reality based on direct experience through entheogenic states of consciousness and energetic awareness. As such, it can be confirmed directly by anyone willing to go through a rigorous process of self-discovery and analysis through highly specific entheogenic methods. It is not a belief system generated through the use of entheogens. It is a direct experience of the energetic nature of reality using entheogenic tools. Beliefs and direct experience are two radically different things, and there are no beliefs in the Entheological Paradigm.

It is a very strong claim to say that something does not contain any beliefs. This is especially true when one is making statements about the ultimate nature of reality. It is a popular *belief* today that *all beliefs are equally valid* when discussing the ultimate nature of reality, and many tout such obviously sloppy thinking as some kind of vaguely feel-good "new paradigm" thought. Many people are of the view that if you believe in something, then, it is, in some sense, true. The corollary to such a view is that it is assumed that all statements about the nature of reality are, by definition, beliefs. In other words, genuine knowledge is seen as dubious, at best, and impossible, at worst, and therefore *all we have are our beliefs.* These beliefs then seem to get support from various experiences that we might have, or we might feel forced to change our beliefs when a given experience does not conform to our previous expectations. Beliefs, therefore, both shape, and are shaped by, our experiences. But at the popular level, at least, questions of ontology and epistemology have fallen by the wayside and there is something of a free-for-all in the reality belief game and much "new paradigm" thinking is a morass of pseudo-scientific mush mixed with incompatible and contradictory spiritual metaphysics. What is sorely lacking is clarity, discernment, and a realistic model of what constitutes "reality."

The question of, "How do we know what we think we know?" is epistemology. The question of, "What actually exists?" is ontology. These questions are intimately related, for how we answer one affects how we are able to answer the other. The Entheological Paradigm provides an ontological answer, coupled with a system of epistemology based on mathematics and a careful analysis of the phenomenology of entheogenic experiences, with special attention paid to non-dual, or unitary states of being.

The Entheological Paradigm is not something that I learned from anyone. Nor is it something that I have intellectually constructed through studying the works and systems of others. It is not based on any pre-existing religious, philosophical, metaphysical, spiritual, or scientific system, though it shares certain concepts and truths with other systems. It is the product of my personal exploration into myself, and the conclusions I was forced to reach about the nature of the self and the nature of reality. Despite having reached these conclusions *subjectively,* I argue that they are in fact universal. In other words, I am claiming to have discovered the genuine truth about the nature of the self and the nature of reality. This is not "my" belief system, nor is it "just my perspective." This is objective truth and others can confirm this for themselves. In fact, that is what is preferred. "Believing" in something is utterly meaningless. Experiencing the truth directly is *the only way to genuinely know reality.* There is no need for beliefs in the Entheological Paradigm.

How I came about the Entheological Paradigm is a complex story. I've shared much of it publicly on "The Entheogenic Evolution" podcast, and will provide a very short summary here. In essence, almost three years ago, I decided that I had been holding myself back and endlessly compromising myself in my life, and found the courage to do something about it. I left everything stable in my life and ventured out on a process of self-discovery. A central component of this self-discovery process was entheogens: in particular, *Salvia divinorum,* Ayahuasca (in the form of Daime), and 5-MeO-DMT. To put it quite simply, what I learned and discovered about myself was that I was God, a "being" that I had no prior "belief" in, and that this being had absolutely nothing to do with any of the religions or spiritual teachings promoted by different human societies and traditions. This was anything but an easy process for my ego to go through. In fact, it was, by far, the most difficult and radically challenging thing I had ever been through in my life. It's one thing for an ego to find out that something it had no necessary belief in existed, but that this being was identical with the self, was quite another matter.

Having my Ph.D. in Religious Studies, I was certainly aware of the widespread *beliefs* in God and a "mystical," unitary reality, as these are common themes in many religions. However, what I also realized, in discovering the genuine nature of myself, is that the vast majority of what all religions have to say about God and the ultimate nature of reality and the self is wildly off the mark, and in many cases, seriously wrong. In truth, it became immediately clear that all those belief systems, religions, and spiritual teachings were mere nuggets of truth wrapped in multiple layers of ego-generated illusion and fantasy.

This was quite startling for me. For one, it meant that all those "possibilities" for which I had once held out an open mind, and in some cases, and yearning heart, were just illusions. It also meant, even more shockingly, that somehow, I had come to understand things that others hadn't – even the so-called "great mystics" and "masters," because it was simply too clear to me where their egos were influencing what they were saying and teaching. Even Buddhism, I found, my personal favorite, was seriously clouded in illusion at many levels. And it wasn't simply a matter of differences in beliefs. It was a difference in our experiences of energy. I found that I could immediately distinguish between ego and truth at an energetic level in my entire being. A visual metaphor might be useful. For those who have eyesight, it is obvious when the light is either turned on or off. You can simply see it. It is not a matter of belief. It is reality. What I discovered in myself was the ability to energetically perceive and experience the difference between when "ego is on" or when "ego is off." What I experienced was that what often passed for "enlightened teachings" was anything but!

I was able to accomplish this in myself because I chose to permanently surrender my ego to my true nature as an infinite energy being (and reaffirm this choice on a moment to moment basis). My ego is still a part of me, but I have learned that is it most definitely *not* me, nor are its ideas or beliefs. In surrendering my ego, virtually everything about me has changed, including my voice, my body, my energy, my thoughts, and my perceptions and experiences. I have experienced what I can only call genuine human liberation. I have freed myself. Through teaching about the Entheological Paradigm, that is what I hope to share with others: a genuine path to true liberation. To get there, though, all illusions must be overcome and released, including those generated by our most beloved entertainers and cultural icons, as well as all religions, spiritual systems, and cultural belief systems. It's a big job, and it progresses one person at a time, one ego at a time. It must be directly experienced by any given individual as this is not something that can merely be understood intellectually or "believed" in. Beliefs and ideas about the nature of reality are completely meaningless. Only by truly learning of your genuine nature as an embodied energy being can you begin to understand the true difference between reality and that which we impose upon it through our own thoughts, choices, and beliefs.

So what is the Entheological Paradigm? It is a complete analysis of reality as the integrated and interrelated expression of a Unitary Energy Being, otherwise known as "God." To put it simply, all of reality is a unified energetic system that is conscious, self-aware, and evolving according to energetic laws. There is no real difference between organic, inorganic, subjective and objective as ALL manifestations within reality follow the same set of energetic rules and laws. Everything that exists is a form of energy and it is all unified within a singular self-awareness and consciousness. The rest of this essay will present an overview of how this works and the role that entheogens can play in bringing about direct experience of the fundamental nature of reality and the process of undergoing self-liberation through awareness and the exercise of personal responsibility.

Consciousness:

Consciousness is not a specific energy, material, or substance. It is an inherent property of reality. In other words, consciousness is not a "product" of biological systems. Biological systems organize and utilize energy in ways that allow for self-referential awareness and expression. Another way of saying this is that all of reality is alive and aware and this property is uniquely expressed in biological beings but is not a product of their biological system.

This understanding of life/consciousness obviates any need for beliefs in "spirits" or "souls." These concepts identify life and consciousness as a *particular* substance, material, or energy, and then give it a name and an identity. Besides there being no scientific evidence for any such "substance" or "energy" of consciousness that mystically and mysteriously "relates" to or "inhabits" the body, there is also no reason to believe in such entities or energies when consciousness is properly understood as a property of reality itself, not a particular energy or construct *within* it.

The Ego:

The ego is a self-referential program within the structure of *human consciousness*. The ego organizes its understanding of what is occurring to it within its energetic field (that which it experiences and senses through the construct of the body) as relationships between what it chooses to identify as its "self" and that which it chooses to identify as "other."   The problem for the ego is that there is no inherent "self" within human consciousness. Therefore, in order for the ego to construct an identity, it must make what are realistically arbitrary decisions.   If there isn't any *real energetic divide between self and other (there is no fundamental "self" with which the ego can identify), then all such designations are by definition conventions and illusions.*

In constructing its sense of self, the ego develops countless energetic programs based on choices it perceives for navigating the artificial/conventional world of "self" and "other."   These energetic programs take the form of habits, beliefs, body postures, movements, vocal expressions, tone of voice, gestures, and behavior patterns in both thought and action.

As the ego is ultimately made up of arbitrary energetic constructs, it continually seeks to reaffirm its sense of self and world and validate the conclusions it has made about the nature and identify of the self.   The last thing that the ego wants to is to be confronted with the reality that, "You're full of shit," as that does not reaffirm its sense of self and world.   In fact, it conflicts with it dramatically.   When such a confrontation occurs, egos have a couple of choices.   One is to pretend that nothing happened, and go about business as usual.   The other is to hold on even stronger to the self-generated illusions, especially through finding others who share similar illusions and allow for group identity, or, embark on an existential crisis that may or may not resolve beneficially.   If beneficial, the individual will find a new state of liberation from the constructs of the ego.   If not beneficial, the ego will simply adopt a new set of beliefs and structures in place of the old ones.

The Difference between Egotistical and "Egoic":

It is extremely important to understand that saying that something is a product of the ego is distinct from claiming that someone is behaving "egotistically."   Saying that someone is being "egotistical" is a social approbation of someone's perceived selfish behavior.   To say that someone's ego is creating illusions and distortions in their experience of reality is not to say that they are being selfish.   For this reason, the word "egoic," as in, pertaining to the nature of the ego, would be a better fit when discussing ego-generated illusion.   For example, Buddhism is well-known for teaching selflessness and is believed to be a path to lessen the ego and free the mind from its illusions.   However, under the analysis provided by the Entheological Paradigm, we can see that while Buddhism might promote unselfish behavior and thinking, it is thoroughly egoic in its constructs of reality. Buddhism teaches, for example, that while there is "no-self," each individual is ultimately a "stream of consciousness" that is "trapped in manifestation" through repeated "reincarnations" until "karma is cleansed" and the individual reaches *Nirvana.*

According the reality of the Entheological Paradigm, none of those claims are true statements about either reality or consciousness. These are just ideas constructed by the ego and are not energetic realities. Consciousness is *only seemingly individuated in biological beings. The evolution of "consciousness" is therefore identical with, first, inorganic, and then later, organic evolution.* This entire evolutionary process is the evolution of the Unitary Energy Being that ultimately *is all of organic and inorganic reality.* This One Being is already *every being.* Living beings are not expressions of a "stream of consciousness" that is "trapped in manifestation" in a linear series of individuated evolving forms. There is no energetic corollary in reality that equates with these illusory concepts. As such, these concepts are constructs of the ego. In essence, Buddhists do not understand either consciousness or the nature of biological evolution and have covered over their lack of understanding with a spiritual metaphysics that has no basis in reality, despite their teachings of "selflessness".

But aren't these concepts generated from the experiences of mystics? Didn't the Buddha experience these things? Don't some people recall past lives?

These are all possible questioning rejoinders to the claims made above. Certainly many people have had "past life" recollections or experiences, so there seems to be some curious data present. However, even specific memory recall does not provide evidence of "reincarnation" of an individuated stream of consciousness. Given the reality that there is only one being that is manifested as all living beings simultaneously, there's no reason that data from one manifestation couldn't be accessed by or transferred to another manifestation. The more interesting question is more along the lines of: why? For what purpose? Seeing that all of reality is the expression of one being, it would seem that that being is, in a very real sense, playing games with itself. It's going about pretending to be "self" and "other," when it is, in truth, All. Any ego that chooses to see itself as anything less than "All" can experience and perceive any myriad of fun "reality games." The possibilities are endless.

So a "past life" experience doesn't preclude other possibilities, including the understanding that there's really only one being "pretending" to many beings at once (and over time). The "experience" does not prove a "reality." It is also important to keep in mind that the Buddha, as a historical person, took many of his teachings from the cultural milieu in which he lived.   While his teachings challenged many of the great assumptions of the Brahmins, including their assumption of the immortal soul or self (the Brahmanic *atman* versus the Buddhist *an-atman)*, he never questioned their teachings on reincarnation and karma (though he rejected the idea of incarnating into stratified social and economic castes), which is why Buddhists had to explain (quite problematically, and to my mind, quite unconvincingly) how a non-existing self is reincarnated via karma by means of a "stream of consciousness."   Here, Buddhists are showing an egoic attachment to the idea of *individual spiritual and conscious evolution.* They also hold onto an egoic idea of some kind of end "release" or "extinguishing" of repeated incarnations and define this as "liberation." That is pure ego projection and rejection of reality as it is experienced here and now, in all its perfection.   Any notion of getting "out" of reality is pure ego-fantasy.   Thus, Buddhism may teach selflessness, but as a "religion," it is purely egoic in nature.   What redeems Buddhism, at least at the practical level, is that it also comes with numerous meditative techniques for stilling, calming, and clarifying the mind, all of which can be quite beneficial for individuals.   These techniques do not necessarily produce "enlightenment," however, and certainly not in the sense of *Nirvana* as being a final extinguishing of endless linear individuated incarnations.

God, or the "Unitary Energy Being":

It might be construed that the use of the word "God" is meant to imply a specific religious or theological view.   This would be incorrect. God is described within the Entheological Paradigm as a Unitary Energy Being, which is quite distinct from any religious construction of a mythical being that stands outside of or beyond its creation.   God, as a self-aware energy being, is reality itself.   Energy, as we know from physics, functions according to energetic principles, and as such, can be expressed mathematically.   Mathematics are universal descriptions of energy: math is not bound by any culture, religion, or belief system.   Math, however, contains its own rules: these are the rules of energy and the transformation and expression of energy.   Reality is mathematical in nature.   It is energetic in nature.

"Objective" science has grouped mathematical and energetic descriptions of reality into different areas of focus and study: physics, chemistry, biology, geology, ecology, etc., all of which are able to map and describe patterns of transformation of different spectrums and conglomerations of energy.   However, when we look across scales, what we find is that the mathematical proportions of geometry, symmetry, and fractal mathematics hold across all levels of reality.

When "consciousness" and "life" are understood as expressions of energy, it is easy to see that here too we find geometry, symmetry, and fractals. Physically, living beings are all geometric and fractal energetic constructs. Yet these patterns of energy extend into behavior patterns, choices, thought patterns, means of expression, etc. All living beings exhibit patterned thought and behavior. With complex beings, such as humans, it is easy to see that our "small" behaviors, choices, and actions, share similar patterns of thought and reaction to our "big" behaviors, choices, and actions. In other words, though it might seem a bit abstract to refer to behavior as a fractal, in the sense that fractals are iterations of repeating patterns across different scales, then the energy starts to become clear. The "little things" reflect the "big things" because they're part of the same ultimate pattern.

We also know that our heart, the immediate physical source of our life energy, emits an electromagnetic field that extends indefinitely beyond our bodies. That electromagnetic field is holographic in nature and is powered by the fractal iterations of our heartbeat. Humans, as well as other living beings, are, quite literally, living fractal energy beings. Even our DNA is structured as fractal patterns!

Why is everything that exists a geometric/fractal pattern of energy? Because the Unitary Energy Being that is all of reality is *a fractal energy being*. This fact is reflected in the particular and "individuated" manifestations of this one being, which we call, from the human perspective, the objects, beings, and occurrences within reality. The only limits within reality are the energetic limits that are inherent to energy itself (which we tend to call physics, etc.), or those that we impose through our beliefs, ideas, and choices, which may or may not be congruent with actual reality.

What this all means is that the only limits to recognition and experience of unitary being are the limits imposed on the self by the ego. In other words, the one and only thing that prevents anyone from directly experiencing themselves as the Unitary Energy Being that they are is their ego and the beliefs, ideas, and illusions that the ego uses to artificially construct its sense of self. It's actually all quite simple. There is no need to introduce complex metaphysics, religion, or spirituality into the picture. It's a simple energetic reality. And as such, the solution to the problem of "separation" is energetic in nature. To be clear, this is NOT a "spiritual" or even a "mystical" issue. It is an *energetic* issue. Once this reality is understood as such, all religions and spiritual traditions can be seen for what they are: obsolete egoic constructs that are not able to deliver on their promises of liberation or salvation because they are based on energetic illusions that in fact *create* the separation they claim to overcome!

Entheogens:

Once the projected illusions, false beliefs, and ideational and behavioral constructs of the ego are understood to be energetic in nature, then seeking an energetic solution becomes a natural and effective choice for addressing the problems created by ego.   And rest assured, ego creates all kinds of problems! How could it be otherwise, when, in principle, ego functions to create artificial constructs of the self and protect these constructs from anything that challenges them? That is an energetic recipe for drama, conflict, violence, hate, fear, judgment, jealousy, rage, victimization, self-pity, indulgence, and on and on. On the positive side of things, it also creates an energetic recipe for questioning, challenging boundaries, exploration, inquisitiveness, inventiveness, and all manner of ways of engaging the world to satisfy our ego's curiosity about the objects of its experience. However, as exceptionally able embodiments of the One, we are intelligent enough to pursue the benefits of our nature without the drawbacks. To do so, however, we've got to get beyond our egos and their reactionary and illusion-projecting nature.

The central key to such a liberation and unleashing of human potential is entheogens. The word, "entheogens," means, "generating the experience of God within," and is meant as a substitute for the more general term of "psychedelic."   I prefer the term entheogen to psychedelic, personally, but perhaps, for my purposes, an even better term might be something along the lines of *energen,* to indicate the idea of "generating the experience of energy." This is what I have come to understand is the primary function of entheogens or psychedelics: they alter our ability to perceive and experience energy. At peak moments, especially of extraordinary medicines such as 5-MeO-DMT, they allow an individual to experience the immediate nature of infinity energetically. This is what might be called a "union with the Infinite," "being one with God," or "being pure consciousness/energy."

Rather than terms such as "enlightenment" or "awakening," the most powerful of entheogenic experiences can be more readily understood as being full energetic openings or expansions. Such experiences are what are traditionally labeled as being mystical in nature. Different mystical traditions have advocated different techniques for reaching such seemingly rarified states of consciousness, from years of meditation, to the traditional use of entheogens. Some traditions, such as Hinduism, Buddhism, and Taoism, have developed sophisticated symbolic systems to describe and harness the energy of such experiences, and structured them into teachings of "subtle energy." These teachings are often combined with other aspects of the traditions' belief systems, and while practical, in some respects, are also made obsolete by a more grounded understanding based on the bio-energetics of the human body rather than ideational realities of a "subtle," yet, unseen body or realm.

Hinduism, for example, teaches that there is a *kundalini* serpent at the base of your spine that you can mentally coax along the axis of your subtle energy centers, which are *specifically understood to be independent of your actual physiology*. This is ultimately a mental energy trick – a way of playing with the mind to move energy. It can be effective. It is also unnecessary. Entheogens are far more effective in moving energy and hold open the reality of cutting out the "middle man" of mental tricks, symbols, and cultural systems. Entheogens go directly and immediately to the source: your actual energy that is present in your body.

Structurally, entheogens are actually crystalline compounds that function as neurotransmitters. Two very powerful entheogens, 5-meO-DMT and N,N DMT are endogenous compounds in the human nervous system. When we ingest entheogens, these crystalline compounds act at receptor sites in our nervous system and dramatically affect our ability to perceive and experience energy. Perhaps this effect is due to the simple reason that crystals work to focus and amplify energy as a physical property of their geometric structure.

Different entheogens alter our ability to perceive and experience energy in somewhat different ways, but underneath any unique presentation is the universal presence of fundamental energy. *Salvia divinorum* presents very differently from DMT, for example, but both alter one's ability to experience energy. Some medicines are more visual in nature, whereas others are more somatic or kinesthetic. Some medicines can produce high levels of vibrations in the body as the energy works through the biological/energetic system, and others produce slow waves of energy that might feel as though they are pushing one over and smearing one out (a common experience with *salvia*).

Egoic Reactions to Energetic Opening and Expansion:

Egos tend to experience themselves as existing in a state of paradox. On the one hand, egos are often terrified to let go, surrender, and just "go with the flow," and on the other, egos relish and crave the release that comes with complete surrender. At base is the issue of trust. When an ego is trusting, it can let go. When it feels a lack of trust, it holds on to fear, and refuses. It is always ultimately an individual choice.

Virtually any entheogenic experience will require the ego to let go, at least to some extent. Egos that refuse to let go at all tend have what is described as a "bad trip," as the individual is just fighting the energy the entire time and refusing to trust. However, different medicines have different abilities to truly open one up, energetically. Letting go all the way on a small dose of mushrooms, for example, is hardly comparable to letting go all the way on a high dose of 5-MeO-DMT. One can achieve different experiential results with the use of different tools.

The most effective tool for an immediate energetic expansion into one's full energetic state is 5-MeO-DMT, with DMT coming up as a somewhat distant second. Even with the infinite power of 5-MeO-DMT, ego still has a choice, however. The infinite expansion is so overwhelming, especially when one is new to the medicine, that ego can either quickly give up and completely let go, or react in absolute horror and terror at coming so quickly "face to face with God."

Even when ego lets go, however, that is not the end of how ego can affect the experience. If the individual has energetic holdings, in the ways of beliefs, ideas, fears, judgments, etc., these will start to work themselves out energetically within the experience. Ego may have let go, but it is still comprised of energetic patterns. As the infinite energy of one's true being continues to expand, it eventually pushes up against these energetic egoic constructs. At this point, the individual may start to have a deeply introspective experience that can take on the form of visionary awareness. Eventually these patterns will gain the upper hand and even though still "tripping" very hard, most individuals will feel the grip of their ego reassert well before the entheogenic event is over and the medicine ceases to have an effect.

Ego can also play off itself not necessarily in the form of introspective awareness, but of extrospective awareness in the sense of seeing and experiencing seemingly very real "exterior" realities. These realities can either be confusing realms of bizarre otherness, or can take on a more archetypal, educational quality where the ego experiences things as being revealed to it by guides and entities. These are all projections of the self, however, and are a method for the self to communicate with itself through simultaneous multiple role playing (similar to dreams in that the dreamer only egoically identifies with one perspective within a dream but is in fact all the characters and the total environment). It is a trick of the mind in an interior space: an energetic virtual reality, as it were. These realities too will eventually disappear as the ego beings to reassert itself and reconstitute its "normal" energetic and behavioral patterns.

When analyzed carefully, all "visions" can be comprehended as messages from the self, even when seemingly completely "other." This is especially the case when appreciated from the perspective that there is, in reality, only one being, and it is communicating between its unitary perspective and the perspective of one of its individuated selves/egos. Often the game-like nature of the communication also becomes apparent, as well as the intrusions of ego and the ways it attempts to overlay the experience with its own sense of meaning.

In other words, *visionary experiences are you giving yourself what your ego is able to process at that time.*

In the absence of specific visionary imagery, the most common perceptions with entheogens are simply perceptions of energy. This energy usually is of a highly complex geometric and fractal nature. This should come as no surprise, since all of the energy of reality is geometric and fractal in nature. It is from this geometric matrix of energy that visions and visionary content arises. *People with clear egos tend to primarily see the energy and do not have "visions" for they are immediately experienced as self-evident projections.* Clear egos don't provide any energetic constructs for the energy to "bounce off of" and form pictures.

Of far more significance than any visionary content is the experience of energy in the body. Visions are an excellent means of communication from the self to the self, but they can also become an object of distraction and attachment. There are times when individuals can benefit from spending more time energetically "in their heads" in that visual space, but in order to ground into actual reality, individuals must, of necessity, get fully into the energy of their entire being, and that primarily means getting their awareness fully into their bodies. This is the difference between living in fantasyland and actual reality. The difference is crucial and real.

One of the great benefits to working with 5-MeO-DMT versus DMT is that, not only is it far more powerful of an energetic opener, but it is also less visual, though its visual nature can be pronounced. The primary nature of the 5-MeO-DMT experience, however, is the overwhelming feeling of fractal flows of energy throughout the body, and not only throughout the body, but throughout all of reality, as well. The feeling is centered in the body, however, and most especially the heart (the location of the largest electromagnetic field produced by the body). There is infinite balance and infinite perfection to this endless outpouring of this symmetrical energy. It is the pure energy of being. It is radiant. It is love. It is what is. It is the Self.

Most people can't maintain that perfect unified awareness of infinite energy for very long, however, and ego begins to collapse in on itself very quickly, even with 5-MeO-DMT. As this happens, energy flows shift and change in the body. The body is the ultimate vehicle for the expression of the full spectrum of your energy and holds the patterns of everything you ever think and do. Anywhere that your ego has created constrictions in your being, or holdings of fear or judgment or lack of trust, will be pushed and aggravated by the energy of one's infinite expansion. This can cause muscle trembles, vibrations, purging, coughing, crying, laughing: any manner of energetic release and letting go.

It is these energetic releases that we tend to call "healing" events within the use of entheogens. Often, entheogenic healing is performed in the context of shamanism where the language is that of spirits, possessions, purification, etc. Energetically, this language is unnecessary, confusing, and promotes lack of personal responsibility. Each individual is personally responsible for his or her energetic holdings, for they were the one who chose to create it in the first place, and only they can release it. There is no magic or mysticism involved. There are no spiritual energies involved. It is all personal energy in your body/being. The Entheological Paradigm promotes radical personal responsibility for all of one's energy. No one is a victim and there is no one to blame. Everyone is personally responsible for themselves and their energy.

Disassociating from one's energy is a pathway to trouble. The way that we relate to our energy inside our bodies and inside our minds is directly reflected in our exterior relationships with others, and indeed, the entire "exterior" world. Our subjective experience is mirrored by our objective experience and vice versa. Energetically, there is no real boundary. Disassociating from any aspect of ourselves, including supposed "others," is a recipe for energetic imbalance, disharmony, and withholding. It is only by taking responsibility for our energy on all levels that we can overcome our egoic energetic tendencies. And taking responsibility means owning our energy and not looking to others either for salvation or blame, in any way. Each individual is 100% responsible for him or herself.

Symmetry:

A key component of getting to know one's energy is the issue of symmetry and symmetrical movement and expression. I first encountered this key feature of energetic balance in myself in my entheogenic sessions and subsequently observed it in others. I now incorporate this as a primary feature of all entheogenic sessions and insist on it for any client who would undertake a session with me.

My first encounter with symmetry came with my very first 5-MeO-DMT experience. The overall experience was so overwhelming that I didn't take much notice of symmetry that first time. However, upon subsequent sessions with this medicine, I quickly learned that symmetry was a central component of the experience and it was anything but inconsequential. In fact, it is probably the single most important element of energy work with entheogens and its significance cannot be overstated. The fact that there is not a single tradition, shamanic, mystical, religious, metaphysical, or otherwise that mentions the key importance of symmetry is a clear indication that there is something very unique about the Entheological Paradigm, and a gaping hole in our collective traditions that supposedly offer awakening and oneness.

The human body, just like all other biological forms, is structurally a fractal, with various subsets of fractal patterns within it. Early life forms exhibit radial, branch, and spiral symmetry in their structural features. Later, more complex life, exhibits bilateral symmetry as a universal structural feature. This evolutionary development and energetic blueprint allowed for the development of complex nervous systems and sensory organs (energy receivers) with brain, spinal column, and fractal branches of nerves. The overall pattern of the human body, along with countless other species, is one of bilateral symmetry.

What I first discovered in my 5-MeO-DMT sessions, and then shortly thereafter with ayahuasca, was that as soon as my energy opened up and my ego let go and released, my body would instantly behave and move with coordinated bilateral symmetry. With the absence of my ego-generated constraints on my energy, my limbs would naturally mirror each other, and it felt as though my arms and legs were moving in tracks of energy. Not only that, but through the palms and fingers of my hands, I could feel fractal waves of energy connecting my heart, the center of my being, to everything else in existence, that poured out of me in explosive, bilaterally symmetrical forms. When I went into symmetry, there were no energetic barriers and I was in a state of complete unitary consciousness and energetic connection.

The best way my ego could make sense of these experiences, where my arms and legs would flow in fluid, graceful movements as my spine undulated and my voice modulated to very deep frequencies with numerous overtones and harmonics, was to accept that "God" appeared be taking over my entire being and moving my body and using my voice (which no longer sounded anything like "my" voice). It was a long process for me to understand what was happening here, and these events of spontaneous fluid symmetrical movement with alterations in my voice (and consciousness and perception) started intruding into everyday events and situations in ways that deeply unsettled my ego. For a time, my ego was convinced that I might be losing my mind.

What I came to learn with time, patience, and a great deal of entheogenic persistence, was that yes, this energy was indeed "God," but it was also me, though it wasn't the "me" that my ego had constructed as its sense of self. In essence, what I came to understand was that to be human meant to be the perfect bio-vehicle for God to experience reality in. Human beings are perfectly autonomous embodiments of God. All of life is One, as is all of reality. But humans are special, because we have the ability to actually know and experience the truth of this reality. It is the gift of the ego that allows for genuine awakening to our full energetic natures. As direct embodiments of the Unitary Energy Being, we have the capacity to fully know who and what we are as living energy.

Eventually, within myself, there ceased to be any distinction between a full energetic opening and "normal" experience. What had originally presented itself to my ego as an experience between "me" and "God" eventually just became the experience of myself, in all my energy, freed from the limiting confines of my ego and its energetic structures. In essence, I came to know and experience my true nature on a permanent basis.

It was through working with symmetry that this was possible for me, and it is the number one tool I use when conducting sessions with others because the difference is real and immediately noticeable. Non-egoic energy, or one's true, genuine, and infinite energy, is, in the human form, bilateral in symmetry, centered, and balanced. Egoic energy is asymmetrical, non-centered, and imbalanced.

What happens, physically, when someone undergoes a full energetic opening? The immediate physical/energetic response is to lie back and open the arms and legs into a "spread eagle" position. Physically, this is when the body is most open. It is also when a person is most energetically open, trusting, relaxed, centered, and balanced. Anyone who has a full energetic opening and is completely surrendered will automatically and immediately go into this position. Imagine an infinite orgasm that instantly explodes you into pure radiant light as you melt into the fabric of the universe and you can start to get an idea of what I'm talking about.

However, not everyone can maintain this level of radical openness and energetic intensity. If someone chooses to let their ego react, it will always do so asymmetrically. The individual will turn to the side, reach out with one hand while closing the other, open their eyes and look off to the side, or they may start to move from side to side or vibrate. Whenever ego decides to react negatively or with closed resistance to infinite energy, symmetry is always broken in one way or another.

Egos who are struggling to remain open and not resist can still maintain some symmetry, but they tend to exhibit grasping and tension in the body. Ego can hold on by attempting to regulate breathing or through griping the hands. The body remains symmetrical, but it is not relaxed, fluid, and supple. It is rigid, firm, and tense. Breathing is labored, being either too shallow or too deep. Generally, these kinds of body movements and signs indicate any combination of lack of trust, fear, lack of personal permission to let go, or even attempting to over-think or intellectualize the experience.

Egos that manage to completely let go fall into spontaneous movements where the individual may or may not be able to recall what occurred during that portion of the entheogenic session. At this point, ego is entirely relaxed and the individual has completely embraced their genuine energy. When this occurs, arms and legs never cross the centerline of the body. Everything the right hand and arm does is mirrored by the left, and the same for the legs. Individuals will undulate along their spines, but never move from side-to-side. All movements are perfectly symmetrical and mirrored.

Even for egos that let go all the way, the energetic structures of ego will eventually reassert themselves. For those who had been doing spontaneous movement, there is generally an abrupt recognition where ego suddenly intrudes and says, "What in the world am I doing?" This moment is easy to spot as someone will suddenly stop moving, or the nature of the movement will change, or break into asymmetry. You can sense the embarrassment of the ego that suddenly catches itself doing something it wasn't aware of. Hands immediately drop to the chest, or come down to the side. The person clears their throat and asks for a glass of water, attempting to regain "normalcy" through asymmetrical action and interaction. When I'm conducting sessions, that's usually the point where I say, "You're ready for more medicine."

Consciously maintaining symmetry in one's entheogenic practice is a way of keeping oneself open, present, and centered. If someone finds it difficult to maintain symmetry, it can really help to have a coach to offer reminders, or even physically help an individual back into symmetry. For advanced guides, I recommend practicing what I call "energetic mirroring" where both the guide and client take medicine together, facing each other, while maintaining bilateral symmetry. The guide is there to be a mirror for the client to help them maintain symmetry and stay completely open and trusting throughout the experience. Obviously, this only works with guides who are practiced at staying symmetrical and working in this energetic manner. Currently, I am the only such provider that I personally know of who is able to work with people at this level of energetic unity and openness.

When seated, legs should be kept open. Think of how small children sit. They never cross their legs as most adults do (who are much more thoroughly entrenched in their egos and energy patterns). They sit with the soles of their feet touching in front of them, making a diamond shape with their legs. This is an ideal and symmetrical seating position. Sitting with crossed legs in lotus or meditation posture is *not effective* for maintaining symmetry or experiencing full energetic openings. If lying down, legs should be slightly open and never crossed. Arms should be kept open with palms up, either on one's lap, or by one's side. This is what I consider the "neutral" position. Whenever you find yourself breaking symmetry, return to this position (either seated, or laying down). If you find yourself moving in bilateral symmetry, go for it – but don't think about it. Just feel your way through the movement and breathing. Any time your break symmetry, however, return to the neutral position and wait for the energy to move you.

While maintaining symmetry, it is most effective to set one's resolve to not act from one's ego. This means choosing not to move, speak, or do anything "normal" during the course of the medicine session. When the ego is "quiet" and not acting out, it is much easier for one to feel the flow of symmetrical energy that is the source of being. Once that genuine energy opens up and starts to flow, movement, vocalizing, and other activities are common. However, these are not the actions of ego. They are the actions of genuine energy. Experiencing the difference is the first step in learning how to recognize the difference between ego energy (self-constructed illusion) and genuine energy (reality) in all contexts, not just entheogenic sessions. This, however, is where it begins.

I have been told that yoga originally developed from spontaneous, fluid, symmetrical movement. It is also highly likely that yoga developed as a system of techniques to mimic the entheogenic experience (meaning that use of entheogens was historically precedent and yoga a later derivative). Whatever the roots, various yoga traditions, as they are practiced today within Hindu and Buddhist cultures, are a far cry from fluid, symmetrical movements. Most yoga and meditation postures, both within and without the trantric traditions, are either asymmetrical in nature, or feature crossed legs, arms, or hands and fingers. This is a clear indication that these traditions are not fully tapping into the nature of genuine energy but are still dealing with contrived, egoic projections of energy. Keep in mind, again, that a full energy opening *naturally* comes with bilateral symmetry in one's energy and body. The fact that these traditions don't teach bilateral symmetry indicates, by necessity, that they do not teach about full energetic openings. Given that a deep level of awareness and understanding of one's energetic nature as a bilaterally symmetrical being is necessary for a genuine experience of reality, any tradition that teaches "enlightenment" or "awakening" through asymmetrical postures is simply missing the mark and still embedded in ego and the energetic constructs of ego. This is a simple energetic reality.

Opening to the full potential of entheogenic experience means going beyond what religious and spiritual traditions are able to offer.

Meditation and yoga are certainly effective means for altering consciousness, and can help produce better health, wellbeing, and personal happiness and clarity. However, they are limited and are often structurally asymmetrical. Moving into spontaneous symmetry means moving beyond all the confines and structures of all the products of the ego, including our most cherished spiritual traditions. Working with entheogens is a different modality than meditation and yoga, and therefore is in need of its own methodologies. While there is some overlap, the differences are significant. As practical energetic tools, entheogens make a level of clarity and liberation available that nothing else can provide. *They are the method.* Everything else is a substitute and imitation.

Taking Responsibility:

Using entheogens and having "mystical" experiences are fundamentally useless if one is not seeking to integrate their experience of energy into everyday, ordinary reality, and working to take responsibility for the self here and now. The truth of our being comes with both tremendous freedom and tremendous responsibility. Given that each individual is an embodiment of the One, right here and right now, how that individual chooses to be and act is completely a personal choice. All individuals can be true to themselves and their genuine energy, or not. It is always a personal choice. All choices come with consequences. That is reality. Each one of us is a fully autonomous version of the Unitary Energy Being. Everyone is God, and God is energy. That's pretty liberating.

This fundamental truth resolves all existential, spiritual, and metaphysical questions. Any system of belief or "knowledge" that claims that a human being is anything less than a full and complete embodiment of God is an ego-generated illusion, pure and simple. That means that virtually nothing of what any religion has to say has any real weight or value for humans – they are fantasy systems. It also means that no one has a soul to save, a mind stream to evolve, or some other perfected world or state to get to. Reality, as we experience it, here now, on planet Earth, is what God is doing. This is it. Any talk about "other realms" and "higher states of being" is pure nonsense and promotes ego-generated irresponsibility and illusion. *This is it, so get real.*

It also means that if you want to "wake up" or "be enlightened," all you have to do is relax your ego and let your energy open up, and then learn how to take full responsibility for yourself and your ego. The most effective means for doing so is using entheogens, but this is a practice that applies to every moment of every day. We are continually presented with opportunities to either act from a place of genuine energy, or act from a place of egoic attachment, projection, fear, and desire. Since so many people have no idea what that difference is, it can be hard to begin. It comes down to something simple, however: the truth. When you chose to act from a place of energetic truth (not "truth" in the sense of what you think you know), you act with genuine energy.

Unfortunately, egos use all kinds of methods to avoid acting from genuine energy. It is very rare that people give themselves permission to "be themselves," and even if they do want to give themselves that permission, they probably have no idea who they actually are or what "being themselves" means. Egos are firmly attached to their sense of identity and don't want to give it up. Egos hold onto culture, religion, tradition, politics, the teachings of their beloved icons, and all manner of ideas of right and wrong, good and bad, proper and improper, to structure how they choose to identify and express energy. In an attempt to "fit in" to a society, culture, family, etc., an ego takes on the patterns and projections of the other egos around it. Children quickly learn how to mimic and master the ego games their parents and community members model for them. They learn how to identify and believe. They learn how to curb their natural energies to "fit in" and "be a good person," generally according to local, and ultimately relative, standards. Ego then gets attached to all of these ideas, practices, and patterns, as that's how it makes sense of itself and its world.

Genuine energy that is not released authentically will always find other ways to try and escape and discharge, or will force ego to create more and more elaborate energetic structures to try and hold it in and sublimate it. For example, humans are sexual creatures. Sexuality and all that comes with it is a natural part of our energetic make-up and is something that needs to be expressed in order to have healthy, balanced energy. Most religions place all kinds of bizarre restrictions and taboos on sex and sexual activity, often placing the strictest requirements on those who would get "close to God" or "be holy". This is highly distorting of natural human energy, however, and the consequences can be severe, such as with epidemics of celibate Catholic priests sexually abusing young boys. In the eastern tantric traditions (tantric traditions as currently practiced in the West have almost no actual relationship to traditional eastern tantric practices), sexual energy is recognized as a means of altering consciousness, but even there, sex has been turned into a largely symbolic and mental process. While tantric practitioners may have avoided the abuse problems of Catholics, by making sex a mental, as opposed to genuine physical, process, tantrics are not fully engaging with their full spectrum of energy and are operating more in their minds than their bodies. In other words, these practices are tending to push them into rarified and sublimated "mystical," ideational realities, rather than living in actual reality, here and now, in their bodies, in their lives, and with their genuine sexual energy.

So we are all free to choose how we think, what we "believe," and how we act. All of these choices bring consequences. Choices that are made with clarity and centeredness in regards to one's energy are choices that bring the best possible results for the individual because they are in alignment with reality, rather than what we choose to think or believe about reality. Genuine energy is often in complete disagreement with egoic energy, however, so making choices authentically can be difficult. Operating from genuine energy means not being concerned about what others think of one's choices or actions. Choices are made and actions are undertaken because the individual understands that such choices and actions are authentic for them at that time, and living true to oneself means being true to one's awareness of energy. When this is lived fully and completely, there is no one to blame and no one can claim to be a victim. Reality has its natural limits and consequences: this is the nature of energy. But within the possibilities presented to us, we are always free to choose. We can conform to what others expect of us, or what our ego expects of us, or what we know is true for ourselves because we are fully aware of the presence of our genuine energy in our body and what it is asking of us.

Trust and Liberation:

It all comes down to trust; trust of the self, trust of one's life and one's energy. Its as simple as trusting your heart beat, or trusting your breath, and trusting that when you act in congruence with your heart, you know you've made the right decision for yourself, no matter what the consequences. In the end, what we're talking about is liberation from fear. Liberation from fear of being oneself. Liberation from the fear of reality. Liberation from the fear of life and the fear of death. Liberation from the fear of succeeding or failing. Liberation from trying and relaxing into infinite nature of being, right here, right now.

Only you can trust that you can be yourself and take the responsibility and courage to live your true energy.

Digesting *The Spirit Molecule:*
Is DMT Inter-Dimensional Rocket Fuel
or a Reflection of the Self?

The Spirit Molecule is a fascinating new film by writer and director, Mitch Schultz, that recounts the tale of the pioneering research conducted by Dr. Rick Strassman and his study of the action of DMT on a collection of research volunteers. Strassman's work was radical for the simple fact that it was the first study using human subjects to probe the actions of a psychedelic compound in the U.S. in nearly a generation. Since the time of Strassman's work, limited forms of psychedelic research have resumed in the United States, though no further research has been conducted specifically on DMT in humans.

Strassman's study itself was very basic: give people intravenous DMT injections and then measure such things as blood pressure and heart rate. Though not a specific area of research for the study, what quickly became the focus of the work was the fascinating reports subjects made of their experiences. The subjective effects of DMT became far more captivating than the physiological responses, and Strassman and his team went to great lengths to document what volunteers had to say about their experiences.

The film, *The Spirit Molecule*, brings together a wide array of contributors to reflect on the nature of the DMT experience and what it may or may not reveal about human consciousness, diving into the deep questions of: what is the nature of reality and what is possible within the far reaches of the human mind? In the film, subjects of the study recount their tales of DMT experiences and various experts from psychologists to mathematicians chime in with their ideas, pondering the question: what is really going on here?, including Strassman's own reflections on the possible relevance of theories of dark matter and multiple universes.

The views discussed in the film, especially in the last third, where different individuals give their perspectives on the question at hand, are far from uniform. If we were to ask the question: what is a working model for DMT experiences and how does it relate to human awareness?, we would not receive a consistent answer from those interviewed in the film. Rather, we are given possible models, possible answers, and ultimately, more questions to ponder. If one were looking for a clear and decisive answer as to what is the true nature of the DMT experience, this film would provide many different possible avenues of explanation, but no coherent, overall model. There is general consensus that "science" plays a role in determining what is happening, but we aren't provided with a clear idea of just what that role is, or how all the views being discussed in the film may or may not be amenable to rigorous scientific analysis or verification.

The problem is that DMT experiences are neither easily explained by current scientific models of reality or consciousness, nor explained away as merely the action of a "drug" that produces subjective "hallucinations." And even if we can develop an understanding of what's going on in the brain, it doesn't necessarily help us to understand what is subjectively occurring within the DMT experience itself or explain why people are having such a wide variety of novel experiences. When it comes to the question of the brain, many interviewees in the film fixate on the pineal gland and the hypothetical role that it might play in the production of DMT endogenously in the human body. It is important to note that this proposed role of the pineal has not been verified and therefore these discussions of the pineal gland and its potential "spiritual" properties are speculative.

Toward the end of the film, Strassman discusses his own shift in thinking that occurred as a result of the accounts of subjects in his research. Somewhat to his surprise, he found that numerous subjects reported encounters with other beings, apparent travel through space, glimpses into other realms, and several experiences that appeared either similar to or identical to "classical" mystical experiences, being the dissolution of the distinction between subject and object. As Strassman himself puts it, it dawned on him that he was "dealing with a spiritual phenomenon." Despite his best attempts to fit these experiences into a standard psychological model, he just couldn't. He states:

> It started seeming to me that what was happening with DMT, particularly with respect to some of these reports of entering parallel or alternate or freestanding realms of existence, that indeed was what their consciousness was doing. The chemistry of their brain, which is the organ of consciousness, was being changed by DMT in such a way that they could receive information that we can't receive normally.

> What I was doing early on when I was hearing these reports was interpreting them, calling them psychological or brain chemistry aberrations or whatever. There was a part of the brain that was

being dinged that was responsible for the alien appearance phenomenon.

To discount the phenomena as hallucinatory or imaginary – I think it is maybe more useful to look at it as a mechanism of action – if it is real, perhaps, how does it work?

Using DMT as an explanatory model, as a kind of mediator between our consciousness and a consciousness of a non-corporeal kind of reality, is kind of handy.

Though not elucidated to any great extent in the film, Strassman's working theory is discussed at some length in his book, *DMT: The Spirit Molecule*. There, he discusses in greater detail the idea of "channel dark matter," which in the film is discussed as follows:

You know, there are parallel universes, it seems. At least, that's a theory in modern physics. There is dark matter – a huge amount of matter of the universe, maybe as much as 90-95% or more. As radical as an idea, it's just a logical extension, in some ways, of instead of using a machine to see more than we normally can see, we're using the brain.

Strassman's solution, then, is to turn to current ideas in cosmology to provide an explanation for what may be occurring in DMT experiences. It is important to note, however, that cosmological theories of "dark matter" and "parallel universes" are two separate, and unrelated, theories or idea sets. It is also important to note that both theories are placed within the realm of *theoretical physics*. Dark matter is a theoretical construct to account for why a large portion of the assumed mass of the universe is "missing," and parallel universes is a theory to account for the effects of quantum indeterminacy and probability. They are not related to each other directly, and, especially when considering parallel universes, are not uniformly accepted by physicists. Parallel universes is only one proposed solution to the quantum problem, and though such prominent physicists as Stephen Hawking and others currently support it, other physicists point out that it is still only a theory and *there is no physical evidence whatsoever that supports this theory*. It is therefore problematic when non-physicists turn to highly contested physical theories to support a specific model of consciousness, especially when physicists themselves are generally uncomfortable with such a supposed connection to questions of consciousness.

If the human brain, when bathed in excess DMT (as opposed to the normal amounts of DMT that are endogenous to the human nervous system), can perceive alternate realities and other beings, then why does this only occur for some subjects, and not others? This is a very serious problem with this model, for if we are considering DMT as producing a certain action or result within the brain, why is it that this only occurs on some occasions and not others? If it were merely a mechanical action, then the results should be somewhat uniform, or at least, more uniform than what the data suggests. For example, we know that if we put enough rocket fuel in the rocket, it will adequately lift off and go into orbit. However, when it comes to DMT, the proposed fuel to human inter-dimensional travel, there is no guarantee of contact with beings or other realms. So here we have a very interesting problem: why does it only produce such experiences on occasion and not reliably? This is a question that the mechanism model does not, and cannot, adequately address.

As a theory, it must be understood as, at best, incomplete, for there are obvious factors and results for which this model cannot account or provide an explanation. There is something missing, and that something is clearly related to the individuals themselves. If one individual takes DMT and experiences beings and other realms, and another doesn't, then there is something more going on here than DMT launching consciousness "out" of the body and initiating inter-dimensional travel and contact. The parallel universe/dark matter theory simply doesn't account for the data. In fact, it doesn't provide an explanatory model at all, for it cannot address this very basic question of why results differ. An adequate theory needs to account for all available data, and this theory doesn't, let alone the problems of relying on unconfirmed physical theories (as stated above) to base a theory of consciousness upon.

Though various speculations are given in the film, Strassman's theory comes the closest to providing a working model for what is occurring in DMT experiences, at least as regards how it may relate to scientific knowledge and understanding. It doesn't work, however, and is only presented in cursory, speculative form. As such, it serves its purpose in the film: to open up questions and discussions concerning the nature of DMT experiences. The film does not purport to give definitive explanations but rather food for thought, and as such, it delivers with a well-edited, visually stimulating, and intellectually challenging documentary. If one is looking for specific answers, however, *The Spirit Molecule* does not pretend to provide them.

Can these experiences be explained, and if so, what does that tell us about human consciousness and the nature of reality? I am convinced that they can, and that we can reach definitive conclusions about human consciousness, being, and the nature of reality. To demonstrate this, I will provide a clear analysis of some of the material presented in the film; in particular, the accounts of the study subjects' experiences. This will not be comprehensive, as there is a great deal more data available in Strassman's book, but it should be enough to be illustrative of the main arguments that I will make. Remember, the strength of a theory or a model is its ability to account for all the data provided. I've already pointed out above how the "dark matter/parallel universes" model fails to do so. In applying my own model of the Entheological Paradigm to the material presented in the film, we will see that all variations and experiences are accounted for within a concise model of human consciousness and the nature of reality.

At the heart of the Entheological Paradigm lies the "mystical experience," or the individual experience of identity with all of reality. In simple terms, it is the experience that "everything is *One*" - all of reality is, somehow, the true nature of the self and identity. Any genuine theory of the nature of consciousness or of reality has to deal with the mystical experience, as it is undeniable data that must be accounted for. If the mystical experience can be understood as consistent with scientific knowledge, then we have the beginnings of a model for understanding the nature of reality as both a direct subjective experience as well as an objective object of study.

In what follows, I will provide a brief overview of the Entheological Paradigm and then demonstrate how this explanatory model can be applied to the specific cases of DMT experiences as recounted in the film. As a model, it is psychological, empirical, physical, energetic, and ontological. It also allows for predictions, specific observations, and definitive conclusions and interpretations. First, an overview:

- All of reality is one, unified, energetic system.
- The energetic system of reality is geometric in nature: primarily, it is fractal in nature.
- Consciousness/life is not a product of physical reality: it is the organizing principle of reality itself.
- Consciousness/life is unitary in nature: there is only ONE consciousness.
- Reality can be understood as a collection of energetic permutations and transformations of one unified awareness or being.
- Reality is itself what we may call "God" – Reality is the "Supreme Being"
- The only "individual beings" that exist are physical in nature as they are the result of numerous energetic changes and transformations within the unified energetic system.

- Evolution is the process through which the Unified Consciousness embodies itself in relatively discrete "vehicles" or apparently "individual beings."
- Human beings, as self-aware vehicles, are the most advanced evolutionary beings that we know of in that we have the fullest capacity for self-awareness and self-expression. Humans are the epitome of evolution and the fullest expression of "God" in physical, embodied form.
- There is no such thing as "disembodied" beings as all beings are by definition, embodiments of the One in physical form.
- The evolution of physical beings has also been the evolution of the expression of the consciousness of the One through long processes of energetic transformation. The evolution of physical reality is necessary for the evolution of conscious beings.
- The human ego is necessary for the evolution of individual self-awareness.
- The human ego can be described as a collection of energetic patterns. These patterns comprise our ways of thinking, beliefs, habits, reactions, and behaviors. Together, these patterns comprise the egoic sense of "self" and form the basis of "normal" human identity.
- In the mystical experience, the limiting energetic patterns of the human ego are transcended and humans are able to have direct experience of their true, infinite natures in that they are able to identify with "everything," for that is the true nature of identity (ie, all of reality is one Unified Consciousness).
- The individuated human ego is therefore a construct and is not fundamental to identity or being. It is merely a collection of energetic patterns.
- The primary role of the ego is to create a specific sense of "self" that is contrasted with what is constructed as being "not self" or "other." In mystical states of consciousness, this divide between self and other is transcended as well as the appearance of relative objects of awareness so that perception itself no longer divides experiences into self and other. All that remains is unitary experience where "all is One."
- When the human ego is stressed or challenged, it can either surrender and dissolve, allowing the individual to experience the unified nature of being directly, or it will use any patterning at its disposal within its repertoire to create a sense of self and other and thereby maintain a sense of separate identity.

- Psychedelic drugs, such as DMT, are best understood as "energetic openers" in that, through ingestion, the compounds themselves alter one's ability to perceive and experience the energy that comprises one's being. In other words, they make it possible to experience the fundamental energetic nature of being.
- The ego, as a collection of energetic patterns and habits, can either be transcended with the energetic opening provided by psychedelics, or it can react by creating artificial, self-projected energetic impressions of self and other through a reactionary attempt of "self preservation" to maintain a sense of individual identity.

We are now almost ready to consider the examples of DMT experiences from the film, with one major caveat: we don't have access to subjects' immediate physical responses during their DMT experiences. Remember that the Entheological Paradigm is, among other considerations, physical. The basic premise is that egoic constructs and patterns are reflected in an individual's physical body as the body and mind function together as a unified energetic system. When it comes to psychedelic experiences, the actions of the ego have an immediate influence on the actions and motions of the body. For example, someone whose ego is reacting with fear to the psychedelic experience will demonstrate this fear in the body: assuming a fetal position, gripping the hands, moving the eyes about in erratic patterns, labored breathing, etc. If someone is struggling and not "letting go," their body will largely show this fact. Furthermore, someone who is trusting and allowing will generally have a body posture that reflects this openness and trust: open hands and arms, steady breathing, and fluid, symmetrical movements.

The clearest indication of surrender or struggle would be the difference between demonstrations of symmetry versus asymmetry in the body. The more the ego has been transcended, the more likely the individual will exhibit symmetry in the body, including eyesight where the eyes tend to focus directly ahead and movements are along the central axis of the body with energy moving the body in undulating waves up and down the main axis. The more the ego is holding on and struggling, the more likely the individual will exhibit asymmetry in the body, movement from side to side, or tending toward one side or the other, and erratic eye movement. When one learns what factors to look for, one can tell whether a subject is letting go or holding on simply by observing the reactions in the body and no direct subjective account of the experience is necessary. Given that psychedelic experiences are always experiences of energy, one's reaction to that experience of energy is always reflected in the reactions of the body. There is a direct correlation between experience and body reaction.

As an aside, this distinction between symmetry and asymmetry also means that an individual can influence the quality and nature of a psychedelic experience simply through consciously maintaining symmetry throughout the session. In much the same way as consciously smiling can help shift one's mood from unhappy to happy, one can also influence the psychedelic experience by keeping the body symmetrical. It is harder for the ego to maintain control when the body is symmetrical given that the ego most often functions asymmetrically. Maintaining symmetry is a direct method for circumventing the reactionary energetic patterns and holdings of the ego. As a direct empirical observation, this is something that anyone can try out for themselves and see the difference in the quality of their experience.

Given that we don't have immediate access to individuals' physical reactions in the film, we will have to make due without such valuable information. There is still much that can be gleaned from their descriptions of their experiences. It is important to keep in mind that I'm using the interviews as they were presented in the film. Here, the interviews have been edited and therefore they are not necessarily complete. Even so, what we will see is that we can come to a very clear understanding of what kinds of experiences individuals were having and how their egos were relating to the energy of the experience without any need to introduce such concepts as parallel universes, spiritual or disembodied beings, or anything of the sort. What we will instead see is individuals either struggling with or coming to grips with their nature as direct embodiments of the One Universal Consciousness. No further analysis or introduction of metaphysical concepts is necessary. In other words, all the data will be accounted for within the model of the Entheological Paradigm and nothing superfluous or speculative will be introduced. This is the hallmark of a scientific approach.

Perhaps the first question is: how much DMT is enough? Here, my approach is to consider the physical reaction of the subject to the medicine. Early in the film, Cynthia Geist, the DMT study nurse, describes giving a large dose of DMT to one of the study subjects. She says:

He just sat bolt upright in the bed. He opened his eyes and they were dilated and black and I thought he was going to turn his head all the way around and I thought, "Oh my God, I hope he comes back," and he did.

The physical reaction she describes here clearly indicates that this individual had "enough." Energetically, the individual is experiencing the rapid and overwhelming energetic expansion that is the DMT experience, and the body responds appropriately. One of the participants, Antonopoulos Spiros, a yoga student, describes this energetic expansion as follows:

> *You're counting down, preparing for your death, waiting to surrender . . . Then there'd be a hum, and the hum would get louder and louder to the point where it broke apart everything that I was or knew, and it got louder and louder until I had to surrender to the sound . . . and then you were there.*

Another participant described the energetic onset as an energy moving up his central column and then effectively exploding out of his head. Though the exact experience is unique to each individual, the overwhelming sensation of energetic expansion is quite clear and is always reflected in an individual's body.

Let us now consider the more detailed case of Susan Blumenthal, a writer who served as one of the subjects in Strassman's DMT study. Her account is very revealing, primarily as an example of what occurs when the ego, at first, struggles with surrendering to the experience, and then relaxes and finds some acceptance to the monumental experience that is DMT. However, what is clear is that Blumenthal never completely lets go, for even when she finds peace and serenity within the experience, she is still attempting to intellectually identify what it is that she is experiencing. In other words, she is still "observing" from the perspective of an individual and does not recognize herself within the experience.

Interestingly, a completely surrendered experience does not coincide with what is often characterized as an "out-of-body" experience. According to the understanding developed within the Entheological Paradigm, there is actually no such thing as an "out-of-body" experience. There is what may be described as a "beyond the body" experience where superficial distinctions between self and other are transcended, but this is not "out-of-body." Just because someone doesn't have any specific awareness of their body doesn't mean that they are actually "out" of their bodies. They have just moved their attention to a non-physical or imaginative/energetic focus. Within the Entheological Paradigm, such experiences are identified as being "within" the "Divine Imagination." This is not a specific "realm" so much as it is a virtual energetic environment that is created by the mind when observing itself (much like the "space" of a dream). This "realm" functions as a mirror of the mind where the Self is able to communicate with the self through symbolic, representational, and abstract forms. Such experiences, rather than being "out there" somewhere, are, in fact, "in here", in the individual's consciousness.

Reflecting on the setting for the DMT sessions, being a hospital room with technicians and lab equipment, Blumenthal originally comments that, "There was the whole environment to be overcome, but little did I know that it didn't matter where I was – I wasn't going to be in my body – I was going to be out in the universe . . . you weren't going to be there." She is clearly convinced that she has experienced a radical "out-of-body" experience. Toward the end of the film, she laments that this is somewhat unbelievable, stating, "What we see here is such a tiny part of what is real. I get really frustrated because of course there is no way to prove that where I went was deep space, that I encountered, you know, other entities, other life forms, that exist in this universe." She expresses a hope that one day our society might come to accept that not everything that exists, "exists where we can see it."

However, when we examine her experience in light of the Entheological Paradigm, it becomes quite apparent that Blumenthal didn't go anywhere at all, especially in the sense that her ego does not appear to have been completely transcended and thus "Susan" was present for the majority of her experience, with only brief glimpses of what the experience can be with the absence of the ego. Thus, the expansion afforded by the DMT was mostly held in check by the grasping of her ego and the constructs that she uses, through her ego, to make sense of her experience.

The first clear sign that Blumenthal's ego is struggling with the experience is the high degree of fear she experiences at the onset of her session. Fear is a very common reaction to DMT, but it is not necessarily a determining factor of the experience, if one can transcend the fear and trust what is occurring without trying to make sense of it. Fear is also one of the primary tools of the ego and it is extraordinarily easy for an ego to manipulate an individual through fear. Fear can arise when the ego is unable to make sense of the experience. Given that the ego is comprised of specific energetic patterns, the rapid expansion of energetic awareness that is afforded by DMT makes it largely impossible to fit the experience into previous concepts or experiential referents. In this confrontation, the ego reacts through fear: everything I think I know is being challenged by this overwhelming *otherness*. The very core of one's sense of self is being threatened with non-existence or irrelevance. As Blumenthal states:

> *There was no concept of time. It was so disorienting. I was so terrified. I've never been so terrified in my life to be blasted out of my body, to leave my body behind, to be going at warp speed*

backwards through my DNA and out the other end into the universe.

She is clearly afraid of what is happening to her. Her ego is not accepting, but reacting. Energetically, fear causes contraction, separation, and a need to preserve the egoic sense of self.

Her description continues:

I reached across, and suddenly I'm in the universe, in this huge void, with these beings on the other side, and I put out my hands and this incredible rainbow of pink light went between me and these entities, and I was trying to make it be like a white light, but it was this incredible pink light, this energy of love, this capacity of love that we as human beings have that I was just trying to send to them.

Though she seems to have relaxed some by this point, having overcome the initial terror, she is still operating from an egoic sense of consciousness. Notice her use of language and how it reflects a concept of herself as interacting in this space: "I reached out," "my hands," "I was just trying." There is still clearly a sense of "Susan" who is narrating and structuring this experience and she is describing it much as someone might describe her perspective in an unusual or particularly vivid dream.

One of the primary functions of the ego is to attempt to "maintain control," especially in challenging or stressful situations. Notice how here, Blumenthal's ego is attempting to control the situation by changing it according to her thoughts of how things "should" be within the experience. Upon describing the light passing between herself and these other "beings," she is not content to merely let the experience be. She describes herself as "trying" to make it be a white light, which has some unspoken attachment in her ego as to the quality of such a light. In other words, her ego sees this pink rainbow light, is dissatisfied by it, and reacts by trying to turn it into what we might presume she thinks of as being "pure" white light. This is a clear ego reaction and attempt to control or manipulate the situation, rather than relax and accept what is happening. She also clearly identifies the light, which she first identifies as the "energy of love," and then as the "capacity of love that we as human beings have." These are not identical concepts, with the first being a more direct description of the experience: an energy of love. However, she clearly identifies herself as "human" and these "other beings" as "non-human," and since the light is coming from her and going toward them, she adds on the description that is a representation of the *human capacity for love*. This is clearly all her ego at work, representing her own fears and concepts within the virtual energetic reality that is the Divine Imagination.

Identifying as a *human*, she is having difficulty processing the experience. She continues by saying:

> *I was looking around at my surroundings and trying to understand,*
> *but there were all of these machines, or structures, or things, that I*
> *had never seen before that I had no idea what they were. I was like*
> *a caveman in a computer lab. I didn't have any idea, but I knew in*
> *my intellectual awareness that this was a very advanced*
> *civilization or life forms, or whatever they were, they were so far*
> *advanced from what we know here on earth.*

Notice again the emphasis on the actions of the "I" in this context: "I was looking around," "I had no idea," "I was like a caveman." This is still an egoic identification of "I," as though "Susan" is somewhere actually experiencing these things rather than merely encountering the contents of her own mind and her own energy. She still can't understand what is happening because her experience is not fitting with her egoic ideas of what is. She has to, through her "intellectual awareness," or her rational, egoic mind, determine that whatever it is she is experiencing must be a very advanced civilization. This is all her ego struggling with the experience. She is making every attempt to fit what she is experiencing into some intellectual box of pre-existing ideas that she, "Susan," can relate to from an egoic level. Notice also the difficulty in maintaining narrative consistency. Though her mind is attempting to construct some kind of narrative here, the context and content is simply changing too rapidly and unpredictably for her to adequately construct a consistent narrative.

Her narrative then has another abrupt shift:

> *It was all very, very impersonal, until I got to the space where I*
> *realized that I was in the area where souls await rebirth, and I was*
> *there, and I had been there, so many times before. I recognized it,*
> *and this incredible transcendent peace came over me – I have*
> *never in my life, ever, felt such peace. Everything was stripped*
> *away. Every hope, every fear, every attachment to the material*
> *world, was completely stripped out of me. I was free to just be the*
> *essence of a soul.*

It is at this point where Blumenthal finds some level of relaxation and trust within the experience. Everything that comes before this point indicates fear, struggle, attempts to control, and attempts to intellectually understand.

This last "scene" does not show a complete release from these tendencies, but it is the beginning of trusting and allowing. Everything that passed before she describes as "very, very impersonal." Given that she was attempting to relate everything she was experiencing to her egoic perspective, it is not surprising that she would find it to be "impersonal." She's showing a great deal of alienation from herself as an embodiment of the One, and therefore finds the massive energetic expansion to be impersonal, alien, and ultimately completely "other." Yet here, in this last scene, she finds the trust and comfort she needs to let go of her normal sense of self, which she describes as "everything was stripped away." This final release only came after a great deal of emotional and intellectual struggle.

But is this really a complete release and transcendence of the ego? It does not appear to be so. Notice how she has now moved from identifying as "herself" to identifying as a "soul." She claims that she knew this "place" and had been there before. It is this sense of comfort and recognition that allows her to relax and be "free." In the shifting virtual world of the Divine Imagination, she was searching for a way to relax and make sense of the experience. It was through letting go of all attachment to material forms and normal identifications that allowed for this to happen. It's as though she's sorting through various fears and ego attempts to understand and finally finds a projection and identification that gives her some sense of comfort so that she gives herself permission to stop struggling with the experience and let herself transcend. But even here she can't just let herself be, and must wrap the experience in the package of "souls" and "rebith," two thoroughly egoic concepts. Notice how she states that, "I recognized it," meaning the "place" in which she found "herself." The deepest recognition is that *the entire experience is the self and there is no "other"*, but she is still identifying as a separate self in a distinct environment. Thus this is not a surrendering of the ego, just a relaxing. There is still the very definite sense of subject and object, and as such, this does not qualify as a mystical experience, and therefore is still defined by projected egoic boundaries and identities.

For Blumenthal, experiences such as the above convinced her of the reality of "other beings" and "other realms" that exist somewhere "out there." According to the analysis presented here, these are all projections and identifications of her ego, however. If she could relax and trust more, and let go of fear and the need to control and identify, then she might be able to move beyond such projections and attachments. Given that these are all explainable as functions or products of the ego, there is no need to accept the claim that these are experiences of things that truly exist objectively within reality. They are real experiences of the ego in a highly energized state, but they are not experiences of real "things." They are projections and attachments. The very language that Blumenthal uses to communicate these experiences tells us as much.

The study participant who is identified as a shaman, Patricio Dominguez, would seem to have a more realistic idea of what is actually occurring in the DMT experience, as opposed to Blumenthal. Where Blumenthal ultimately argues that the set and setting is irrelevant as DMT "blasts you out of your body" and sends you into the "universe," Dominguez takes a more measured approach. Early on in the film, he states, quite emphatically, that set and setting are all important for working with psychedelic medicines. But here, "The set and setting is your internal self. The things that you have learned, the capacities that you have achieved, the conditions of your own psyche and psychology, these are your set and setting." In the language of the Entheological Paradigm, the set and setting are ultimately energetic constructs of your ego. If you hold onto a lot of fear with your ego, then that is what you will experience. If you show a tendency to try and control situations and manipulate what is occurring, then that will reflect in your experience. If you continually think in terms of self and other, then that is what your experience will reflect. The habits of your ego are the ultimate set and setting. Blumenthal's experiences demonstrate this truth quite clearly.

Dominguez seems to have had a very different quality of experience in his session with DMT, and his account comes closer to a full mystical experience, though there is still some attachment to intellectual thought in his account. Overall, his account shows a new appreciation and a shift in perspective, but not necessarily a full mystical expansion. He begins his account with the following:

More and more layers of my humanity start peeling off . . . at some reaches, way in there, there is like the last layer of that which defines you as a human being and it goes "click", and you're no longer a human being, in fact, you are no longer anything that you can identify.

Notice how quickly Dominguez moves from discussing his personal experience to making an attempt to universalize what he has learned in a way that would be applicable to others, whereas Blumenthal's account largely never moved beyond what "I" saw and experienced. Here, Dominguez recognizes that the DMT experience can very quickly move one beyond anything that can be previously known or identified, particularly as it relates to the sense of the self and identity. In other words, he's recognizing that there's something more than just personal experience at work here. In his own words:

In this meteor-like trip through the infinite space of the interior consciousness, up pops up the picture puzzle patterned door, and I'm whizzing through this sucker as if it was nothing, I'm just flying through it, but now I know what the picture puzzle patterned door is: the picture puzzle patterned door is the farthest reaches of your humanity. This is the doorway into what defines you as a human being. When you go past that, you stop being human, to a degree, and the further you go past this point, the further you go from being a human being. But right here, this picture puzzle patterned door is everything – it is what defines you as a human being. It is you!

Within the Divine Imagination, the self communicates with itself through symbolism, metaphor, energetic experience, and visual representation. Here, Dominguez is symbolically recognizing that what defines us as humans is a collection of patterns, which he calls the "picture puzzle patterned door," a symbolic representation of the embodied, egoic self. He clearly has experienced himself as being something that is far beyond this limited collection of patterns, but what that is, he has nothing to say, other than that it is "beyond" what it means to be simply a human being. He has therefore transcended his limited identification as a human individual with an ego and a particular sense of self. This is the beginnings of mystical awareness, but only a beginning. In the language of the Entheological Paradigm, he's managed to transcend his limited awareness and the patterns of being that he identified with as an individual. However, as a caveat, I would add that his final statement that the picture puzzle patterned door "is you!" is more a recognition that this collection of patterns is "you" in the sense of being an egoic being with a separate sense of self. It is "you" in the small, limited sense, but not "You" in the full, infinite sense. Thus this is an experience of transcendence, but apparently not mystical union. The true self, as revealed in mystical awareness, is *everything* – not just a particular manifestation of the self with which you have personally identified.

Our next, brief, example, moves us a bit closer to the mystical experience, but does not quite go all the way into complete union and dissolution of the distinction between subject and object. Here, Robert Weisz, a psychologist, mentions experiencing himself as a form of "witness" to his experience. He states:

There was no "I", just the sense of a witness being suspended in this incredible vaulted space, like a cathedral made out of stained glass of all imaginable colors, unbelievable brilliance and saturation of color, just this amazing pattern in this dome, this gigantic dome, like the size of a small planet. And there were these winged beings, I don't remember exactly what they looked like, but were like angels [said with tone of uncertainty] *– something like angels, that were majestically kind of flying through this space. But there was something about the quality of how they were flying that was unique – I'd never seen anything like it. It was, I don't know, the sense of another realm that was there. My sense was, at some point, this implicit sense, "This is the divine realm, this is the divine realm," and it wasn't like a thought, just this implicit, groking recognition.* (brackets mine)

Weisz has clearly transcended his normal sense of self, leading him to state that there was no "I" within the experience. It might be better put that there was no sense of "Robert" within the experience, for certainly there was some form of witness, and therefore a perceiving subject. However, he's not focused on the identity of that subject and has not wrapped it within a specific notion of himself from a particular point of view. He is, therefore, to some degree, identityless and merely an observer. Yet there is still a distinction between perceiving subject and that which is perceived; namely, the enormous vaulted space and the winged beings that he perceives therein. Notice that he does not claim that these were angels with any sure confidence. In fact, his tone of voice indicates that internally he questions this designation, but he uses it, as it seems to be the best description that he can identify for what he perceived. He also definitively describes this space as "the divine realm," though he does not provide more elaboration on that point.

Out of the accounts we've considered thus far, this is the most straight-forwardly "spiritual." What we can see is that, despite not creating a specific identity for himself within the experience, he is still categorizing the experience according to the constructs of his mind, and therefore still processing the experience from the vantage point of the ego, or constructed sense of self, despite the apparent transcendence of the ego.

The final account that we will consider here is that given by Christian Meuli, a family physician. I've chosen to end with this report as it is the most clearly mystical of all accounts provided in the film and demonstrates moving into a mystical state, the state itself, and then the eventual "downfall" out of the state of complete union and dissolution of opposites. Meuli begins his account with the following:

I thought I'd died. I saw the clouds – Renaissance white fluffy clouds, with God and the angels, and that's what I saw. I thought I

*was dying and going out, but I did take a quick look at Cindy and
at Rick, and they were both there watching, looking very calm, so I
thought, "That's good news, my body looks fine."*

What we can see from this account are numerous prerequisites for a
full mystical experience. Meuli begins by directly stating that he thought
he had died. Passing into a full mystical experience means leaving behind
all former notions of self, which many people describe or experience as a
form of death. Indeed, the onset of DMT is so abrupt, so energetically
expansive, that this is a very reasonable determination: *I'm dying.* One
passes so quickly from the familiar into the totally unknown that the
experience is radically startling to the ego. If one can relax and surrender
to the experience, then it can move into mystical union. If there is any
resistance in the ego, a more superficial, virtual kind of world of beings and
realms is entered as the mind and ego struggle to make sense of what is
occurring and identify "where" the "self" is.

Significantly, Meuli's experience begins with the appearance of
classical "heavenly" motifs, which he describes as being similar to
Renaissance art. There is still content that is definitive and identifiable. An
interesting feature of DMT visions, and for other entheogens/psychedelics
that have a strong visual quality (and is also observable in lucid dreams), is
this "chicken or the egg" kind of paradox. Did the vision of heaven lead
Meuli to think he was dying, or did his thought that he was dying lead to
the appearance of the vision of heaven? The most accurate way to look at it
is to consider that this functions largely simultaneously, for what DMT
makes possible is the direct observation of one's thoughts, projected
outward in symbolic and representational form. As thought changes, so
does the visionary content. As the visionary content changes, so does
thought. The key for letting this process unfold without interference by the
ego is to allow what is being perceived without engaging in normal egoic
responses, as it is the reactions of the ego that tend to short-circuit the
experience. What could disrupt this process here would be for Meuli to
become attached to the vision through desire, or to withdraw through fear.
What we see, however, is that he does neither. He takes a quick look at
Rick and Cindy to confirm that he is not, apparently, in any real danger,
given their calm presence, and he then finds the necessary trust within to
move on to the next stage of the experience. He is able to accept what is
happening and chooses to allow it to unfold without attachment or fear.

What happens next is a classical description of a mystical
experience where all distinction between subject and object is transcended
into one, unifying experience where the subject is able to identify as
"everything." Meuli describes the experience as follows:

So I went into this white light. As soon as I went into it, I lost any sense of being different – any sense of what I was doing, the past, the future – it was absolutely blissful and euphoric, and I just felt like, it wasn't "I" - I was everything – I was the light. There was no sense of separation, no shadows, no differences, no past, no future – it was all present – and white-yellow light.

Here there is no differentiation within the experience. The perceiver and that which is perceived is experienced as being identical. All superficial boundaries and limits have been transcended. The experience itself becomes timeless, eternal, and infinite. There is no fear, no attachment, no striving for anything, no attempt to intellectualize the experience or define it as anything other than what it is: the immediate identity of the individual with the infinite. The individual accepts the fundamental reality that he is everything.

However, this intense level of mystical union is difficult to maintain for very long, especially when working with a medicine like DMT, which is relatively fast acting and of short duration. As we have seen in all these accounts, the onset of DMT is extremely rapid, and despite any descriptions of sudden encounters with other beings and other realms, what is fundamentally going on here is the subject is being exposed to a massive energetic expansion with the potential for allowing one's energy and awareness to extend into the infinite. If the ego gets in the way, a lesser order of experience ensues with beings and realms presenting themselves to the subject. Such phenomena are always the result of egos holding on or attempting to maintain some control or sense of self within the experience. The ego, as a collection of limited energetic patterns, can effectively get in the way of individual expanding into the infinite. Even when the ego does get out of the way, such as in the account given above, the effect is transitory, for as the medicine begins to wear off and the energy of the experience diminishes, the ego will immediately begin to reassert itself. In most instances, the ego is relentless and incredibly tenacious. As soon as it has an opportunity to return, it will, as in the following:

Then I felt myself falling out of this light. And as I fell out of it, I could feel the light was aglow like the sun with flames coming out, lapping out, and I could already feel this tremendous sense of separation.

Many of those interviewed for the film lamented that the rapidity of the DMT experience and its overwhelming nature make it difficult to "bring anything back" from the experience, or makes it difficult to "learn." When we understand DMT as a rapid energetic opener and expander that allows for the entry into mystical experience, we can accept that really there is nothing to "bring back" in the sense that there really isn't anywhere to go. At its most powerful, DMT allows the individual to experience who and what they truly are: *God, the One Being that is Everything.* When understood this way, we can then analyze the event in terms of how successful one was in letting go of the ego or how tightly the ego held on and interfered with the potential mystical experience. As such, DMT is a powerful tool for helping individuals learn how to release, choose trust over fear, choose allowing over refusing, letting the mind open over clamping down through intellectual discrimination, and choosing union over separation. Desiring to "bring something back" is just not an effective approach to working with DMT. It is simply a process of learning how to get out of your own way and receive the gift of directly experiencing who and what you truly are in your most genuine and infinite form.

When working with DMT as a tool for transcending the ego, an effective technique to is take more medicine immediately upon the resurgence of the ego. For example, in the account considered above, Meuli could have taken more DMT as soon as he felt his ego return and the coinciding feeling of separation. Energetically, the limiting structures of his ego were beginning to clamp down on the infinite energetic expansion afforded by the DMT; he was past the peak of the experience. Though still "tripping" fairly hard at that point, it is highly likely that if he were to immediately consume more DMT, he would return to a more expanded state and have another opportunity to experience his genuine nature.

Of course, one can't take DMT all the time, and that's not the point. Using powerful medicines like DMT is simply training and practice. It is a process for learning how the ego limits the expression and experience of the self through its energetic constructs and the choices we can make to allow ourselves to move beyond our self-imposed limitations. Viewing DMT as a tool to visit other realms or encounter other beings is simply misguided and is thoroughly egoic in nature as these are all projections of the ego in the energetic virtual reality of the Divine Imagination. The ultimate power that DMT has as a tool for personal awareness and being is that it affords the rare opportunity to move beyond these illusory appearances and encounter the infinite nature of the self directly and powerfully.

To return to the original question of whether DMT is inter-dimensional rocket fuel or a reflection of the self, it should be quite clear where I come down on this issue. The inter-dimensional rocket fuel hypothesis simply doesn't account for the facts, provides no explanatory model for what is occurring other than vague speculation, offers no predictions or methods of observation or measurement, and relies on incomplete physical theories, at best, and is far more metaphysical than anything else.

A response that I often receive from those who disagree with my system of analysis is that humans have been experiencing spirits and disembodied entities and realms for as long as humans have been around and therefore must be real - indeed, several interviewees in the film make similar comments and claims. However, when we understand that humans have had egos throughout their history, then we can also see that their egos would have had an impact on their so-called "spiritual" experiences. Therefore, the history of "spirits" in human cultures and experiences is no argument for their actual existence. All that it tells us is that the human ego, when confronted by challenging and unusual energetic situations, has functioned in a similar, and predictable, manner throughout human history.

Finding clarity within the entheogenic experience is not easy. It takes work, time, and dedication. It is extraordinarily easy to get caught in one's projections, illusions, attachments, and habitual thoughts and reactions. As I've indicated in this essay, there are methods that can be employed to lessen the possibility of such interference by the ego, with the maintenance of symmetrical body postures as the most direct. It is the mystical experience that is truly at the heart of being, and is the highest potential that entheogens offer for users. In the end, it is a process of learning how to accept what one truly is, and then applying that energetic awareness to all aspects of life responsibly and consciously, not just in the entheogenic experience. Entheogens offer a genuine path to true liberation from the confines of the ego, but the process is not automatic. Free will is never violated by entheogens and one is always free to react however one may like. One must choose to relax, surrender, and let go. And really, that's just the beginning of the process. Everything else is just foreplay.

THE *AVATAR* DREAMHUNT:
Why Psychedelics Make *Avatar* More Sophisticated

There is a scene that is conspicuously absent from both the theatrical release and extended DVD release versions of James Cameron's *Avatar*; the scene of the "Dreamhunt." The inclusion of this scene, as originally depicted in the *Avatar* script and then included as an incomplete scene as a DVD extra in the special edition release, would have lifted the story of *Avatar* to a whole new, and more complex, level. Had this scene been included, the roles of entheogens and relationship to the biosphere would have been a literal, rather than just implied, theme within the film, and would also have been more true to the indigenous roots of inspiration for the film. Furthermore, it would have raised more realistic and complex spiritual questions in relation to the film's primary themes. Additionally, it raises interesting questions about the process of self-discovery and choice of identity. To my mind, it's a shame that the scene wasn't included. Perhaps it was due to time and the economy of storytelling that Cameron chose not to include the "Dreamhunt." Perhaps he considered the scene too controversial. For whatever reason, it didn't make it in. I'd like to consider how the film would have been richer, had Cameron chosen otherwise.

The film, as it is, features our hero, Jake Sully, having to pass one final test in his arduous journey to become "one of the people" and be accepted as a member of the Na'vi. He describes this test as being all important and uses it to justify to Colonel Miles Quaritch why he has to stay longer among the Na'vi and not give in to the desire to abandon his journey into the indigenous and return to Earth to get a new set of legs and thereby end his days of being bound to a wheelchair. We then see Jake transfer his consciousness into his avatar body and the ceremony among the Na'vi commences with Jake being painted with a white paint or clay, in preparation for what is about to occur. However, in the very next shot, Jake is emerging from the roots of the great Home Tree, suddenly accepted as one of the Omaticaya people. We, the audience, are left wondering: What happened? What was the one final trial that Jake had to endure before making this triumphant transformation? What was the act that allowed for him to claim that he had now successfully been "born" a second time, now as one of the people?

The answer, as revealed by the inclusion of incomplete scenes in the extended DVD release special features, is the Dreamhunt of the Na'vi, which, like many indigenous cultures, past and present, includes the ingestion of psychedelic alkaloids. How might the inclusion of this scene have changed our appreciation of the film and its message? Before answering this question, let's consider some of what was included in the film and what it presents to us.

Upon the release of *Avatar*, the entheogenic/psychedelic community was a-buzz with excitement, given the seemingly obvious nods to ayahuasca shamanism and culture within the film. Ayahuasca is a psychedelic brew made by indigenous South American cultures that contains the monoamineoxidase inhibiting vine of *Banisteriopsis caapi* and the dimethyltryptamine (DMT) containing *Psychotria viridis* leaves. When these two plants are combined together, they allow for potent entheogenic experiences to ensue for those who are brave enough to consume the often-nauseating drink. Ayahuasca has been used by indigenous cultures in the Amazon for hundreds, if not thousands of years. More recently, syncretic religious traditions in Brazil, such as the Santo Daime and Unio Do Vegetal have also incorporated ayahuasca-based drinks into their religious practices. Beyond the Amazon, ayahuasca culture and consumption is rapidly spreading around the world.

Entheogenic shamanism and religious-based practices have a long and significant role in human cultures, religions, and belief systems. In some cultures, consumption of entheogens, or plants or fungi that contain psychedelic alkaloids, is a primary feature of the culture and tradition, such as with South American ayahuasca shamanism. In other traditions, use of entheogens has been limited to a select few or a minority of the tradition, such as Sufi Muslim use of an ayahuasca-analogue drink and the proposed use of psychedelic mushrooms by early Christians. Though it is often not recognized in contemporary culture, entheogen use has been a part of human understanding of its place in the cosmos for a very long time. And for many cultures and traditions, entheogens are crucial in the personal quest for understanding the self and identity.

In the film, *Avatar*, there are many elements that are reminiscent of ayahuasca and South American indigenous traditions, though Cameron himself has stated that it was North American indigenous cultures that were the primary inspiration for the Na'vi and their cultural life-ways. We learn in the film that the Na'vi's spirituality is not just a system of belief, but actually grounded in direct experience of their deity, *Eywa*, which is described as the consciousness of the planet Pandora, itself. All living beings on Pandora communicate via electrical signals, which, for plants, is accomplished through the roots, and for animals and humanoids, through their queue, a sinuous collection of neural fibers that, when joined, connect two living beings together directly via their nervous systems. The Na'vi word for this feature of their symbiotic biology is *tsaheylu*. What makes the communication possible is the transfer of consciousness through energy and electrical signals.

With their queues, the Na'vi are able to link their minds to their chosen animal companions, at times creating life-long bonds. They are also able, through linking to the *Tree of Souls*, to communicate directly with the consciousness of their ancestors. The Tree of Souls, which is depicted as a luminescent willow tree, serves as something of a network link-up for the Na'vi, who are able to transfer their consciousness completely into Eywa upon death. This is accomplished by the tree extending the tendrils of its roots out of the ground and encasing a dying Na'vi, providing the most direct link to Eywa. To access these forms of consciousness, the Na'vi link their queues to the luminous vines of the tree.

We are provided with two different scenes in the film where characters link directly to Eywa via the root tendrils: the first is when the Na'vi attempt to save Grace, who has been shot, by transferring her consciousness directly from her human to her avatar body. The second is at the conclusion of the film when Jake willingly, and successfully, does the same, abandoning his frail human body forever and permanently joining his consciousness to his avatar body.

Though obviously a fictionalized and mythologized story, there are important connections to ayahuasca in the Na'vi's relationship to their environment. Perhaps the most significant is the idea that there is something tangible about the people's connection to their environment; something that goes beyond mere "belief" and "superstition." Among ayahuasca using cultures, the ayahuasca itself is viewed as this tangible connection. It is through the medium of the visionary and energetic ayahuasca brew that the people are able to directly connect with what they view as a larger, more expansive environment. The name itself reflects this understanding: *the Vine of Souls*, or *the Vine of the Dead*. Simply, and perhaps misleadingly put, the drink allows for individuals to connect directly with "the spirit world." More precisely, it puts people directly and intimately in contact with a rich experience of energy and consciousness.

Yet even here, there is a contrary message in the film, *Avatar*. At one point, the scientist, Grace, defends her interpretation of Na'vi spirituality by claiming that it is empirical: it is based on energetic neural connections. In other words, it has a physical basis. She issues this argument as a response to the question of "What have you been smoking out there?" thereby implying that an entheogenic/psychedelic practice has less validity than what is offered by scientific proof. Later in the film, when Grace is at the point of death and attempting to transfer her consciousness, she proclaims to Jake that "Eywa is real," and she knows this because she is "with her."

Graces' moment of "belief" comes when her consciousness must pass through the "eye of Eywa." Graphically, the event is depicted in a way that is very reminiscent of a DMT experience. The same holds when Jake must also make the same journey. However, even here, we are presented with a representation that makes the experience less "mystical" than ayahuasca, because it is accomplished through direct physical connection via the root tendrils. Ayahuasca, in contrast, would still seem more "mystical" in that it opens an individual to a private experience of energy and consciousness, and any link of the "vine of souls" is chemical, through ingestion, rather than a physical and direct neural link to the "Tree of Souls."

From the scientific perspective, as presented in the film, there is an empirical reality to Na'vi spirituality, even if it still might be dismissed as "tree hugger crap," as expressed by Jake early on in his journey to becoming a Na'vi. Grace, the scientist, can appreciate what the Na'vi believe because she understands the science behind it. Jake, though immersed in it through his training as a Na'vi, is still skeptical, though admittedly drawn in through his attraction to Neytiri. What, if anything, could truly change Jake's mind?

Apparently, it was the scene that we, the audience, never got to see: the Dreamhunt. Significantly, the set-up for the initiation in the final film is quite different from the scene as it was originally intended. In the finished film, Jake claims that he must go to a ceremony for his final initiation and rebirth as a member of the people and nothing more is indicated. In the Dreamhunt scene, Jake claims that this is his final test, but there is more that is revealed. For one, Grace tells Jake that this will be very dangerous for him and that he is indeed risking his life, for he is to go on a dreamhunt. The ritual consists of the initiate having to eat a worm as well as endure the sting of a scorpion-like creature. The worm is significant as it eats from the "sacred tree," presumably the Tree of Souls, and contains a psychoactive alkaloid. The scorpion provides a potent neuro-toxin that brings the Na'vi close to death. When combined together, the two compounds unleash a powerful psychedelic experience that allows for the initiate to go on a "dreamhunt" and attempt to contact their "spirit animal." Grace is concerned that Jake is about to get himself killed by this unpredictable experience and the chemicals involved.

Jake is insistent that he must go and do this, however, for he has every intention of becoming one of the people. He wants this so badly that he's willing to risk his life on it. It is then that reality sets in: Grace informs him that he will never truly be one of them and will never truly be able to be with Neytiri, for this body in the wheelchair is who he truly is, and his avatar is merely an extension of all of their technology and industry.

Clearly Jake is struggling with this reality and he is torn by his heart and his desire to be with Neytiri and the culture he has fallen in love with. It is then that he admits to Grace that he's been working for the Colonel all along, and that no matter what, the plan is to destroy Home Tree and drive the Na'vi out.

The significance of this exchange is that Jake is now ready for his vision quest in the sense that he has confronted the truth of the situation. Until this point, he had been living in a fantasy, so to speak. Given his identity as Jake Sully, ex-marine and avatar driver, it's true; he can't really be with Neytiri or the Na'vi. He's been lying to them and himself about that. And he's been lying to Grace and the others in the avatar program about his role in their work. The truth has now been exposed. Granted, the Na'vi are not yet privy to all this information, so Jake hasn't been completely forthcoming, but it is the beginnings of honesty and at least internally, Jake is no longer able, or willing, to live the lie. He's beginning to understand that he has to confront the truth and that living in fantasy is a recipe for disappointment and disaster. Confronted by this reality, he proceeds to the ceremony of the dreamhunt.

It is also significant that Jake is willing to die for this. The journey into truth and self-realization is so important for Jake that he is willing to risk his life for it. Though it is not a feature of every entheogenic experience, passing through what is often identified as "ego death" is a highly salient feature of doing entheogenic work. In order for an individual to expand completely into their infinite nature, he or she must be willing to "let go" of everything that they think and believe about oneself: the individual must be willing to surrender completely and, in essence, "die." The physical body doesn't die, however. It is only the individual's sense of self, or ego, that actually "dies" in the process, yet the continuity of the individual's consciousness and sense of being continues. It is when the ego is completely out of the way that the individual can experience the genuine nature of the self and come to a new, more expanded, sense of identity and being. Those who let go of the ego are privy to deep revelations about the nature of the self. Those who refuse to let go and latch onto their fear of dying are doomed to struggle and suffer, and are left at the mercy of their often-confusing visions and psychedelic experiences. To truly do the work requires a deep level of personal willingness and trust.

The ceremony itself takes place in a secluded area of what appears to be Home Tree. After being properly painted, Jake descends into the spiraling roots to assume his place in the center of the circle of those gathered for this crucial ritual. One Na'vi plays a water drum while others chant. Neytiri's mother presents the worm to Jake, who holds open his mouth and extends his tongue to take the proffered sacrament. Then from behind, Neytiri's father brings forth the scorpion, which stings Jake in the back, twice. He has consumed his medicine. It is time for the visions to begin.

There is no direct, physical, neural contact for this vision. Jake is alone, connected to the wider energetic environment solely through the psychoactive alkaloids coursing through his body. He has not attached his queue to any roots or any other living being. He is all on his own. He is on his private dreamhunt.

The effects of the alkaloids come on quickly. The others crouch around Jake as his vision and other senses begin to distort. Jake struggles with the alchemical mix inside him as he begins to journey into the unknown. As the experience deepens, he beings to let go of his struggle, which, in the incomplete scene, is depicted as Jake disassociating from his physical body. His physical body is shown as face down, likely to purge, but his "energetic" or "spiritual" body is shown as sitting on the ground, his arms out in front of him in a relaxed symmetrical posture as his head lifts up and moves into the energetic perceptions generated by the medicine.

As Jake's awareness of himself changes, he begins to ascend. He sees Home Tree as a vast network of complex energies that are continuous with the energies of his body. He ascends up into the vault of the enormous tree, spiraling upwards like the thick branches of the tree itself. Moving ever upwards, his energetic vision expands outwards. Jake is no longer witnessing the tree: he is seeing the pure energy of being. Here, his vision shifts into a vast and complex energetic array that is presented before him symmetrically. Though there is no narration, the import is clear: Jake is merging with the totality. He has completely passed into an energetic state of being and is no longer bound by either his body or his ego, his sense of self. There is nothing but pure energy. He has fully let himself "die" to the experience and is ready for his coming "rebirth".

In a psychedelic or entheogenic experience, this would be considered the peak, or the most intense moment of the journey, where all boundaries dissolve and all things are seen as they truly are: infinite. It is quite common, when visual, for such experiences to be primarily geometric, and highly sophisticated, in appearance. As in Jake's vision, the appearance of bilateral symmetry is extremely common in such visionary experiences, as is evidenced by the preponderance of this theme in both ancient and contemporary visionary art. Radial geometry and symmetry is also quite common, though not depicted here.

Personally, I find the appearance of bilateral symmetry in visionary experience to be highly significant. As I understand it, the entheogenic experience is always an experience of the self, and primarily it is a reflective experience: it is a glimpse into the infinite mirror of the self. As physical beings, humans, or in the case of *Avatar*, humanoids, exhibit bilateral symmetry in the physical structure of their being. This also indicates that energetically, humanoids are also bilaterally symmetrical. Even in an experience that is seemingly "beyond the form" of the physical, the archetypal energetic structure remains within the vision. It is the self observing the true nature of the Self as pure energy, but still within a recognizable geometric form. It is an energetic mirror reflection, infinite, but structured, patterned, and organized.

Phenomenologically, it is very common for highly geometric visionary states to transform into more recognizable forms with the appearance of visionary beings, scenes, and experiences. It is as though the mind is not able to sustain pure geometry, and in order to make sense of the experience, forces it into images that can be related to more directly. In my analysis, this is a result of the ego, or sense of self, that struggles to relate to the pure energetic form of the self, and as a result, starts to project imagery into the geometric matrix in order to communicate with itself symbolically. When confronted with the infinite, the ego struggles and asks, "Who am I?/What is this?" If it can remain within the raw energetic truth, it will accept that the self is the pure presentation of energy. Otherwise, the ego must relate to the energy through visionary content and through imagery. Many entheogen users consider this to be an opportunity to learn about the embodied self and address the question of who one is and what one's place is in the universe.

It is at this point in the scene that Jake then sees his dream spirit animal: *Toruk*. Toruk is a large, fierce, dragon-like creature that has been ridden by a leader of the Na'vi only five other times in their history. In his vision, Jake sees the Toruk and then sees the shadow of the Toruk flying over a devastated landscape, charred with burning trees. Tellingly, we are seeing the scene through Jake's eyes and can see that conjoined with the shadow of Toruk is a rider upon his back, who is obviously Jake. Jake and the "Last Shadow" are one. They share the same perspective. They are one identity.

Jake emerges from his vision, screaming and jolted back into his awareness of his physical body. The dream is over. He tells no one of what he has seen, and he is escorted out of the ritual room and greeted as one of the people. He has passed his test. He has withstood the demands and uncertainties of the vision and is now one of the people. He has died and has been reborn.

In many ways, the scenes that didn't make it into the film would have made the film a more complex one. Though I won't discuss other non-included scenes here, it suffices to say that the many of the nice, clean messages of the film are more complex. Some of the "good guys" don't seem as good or innocent, and some of the "bad guys" aren't as bad as they appear directly in the film. Furthermore, the "pure science" of Na'vi spirituality becomes complicated by the mystical/shamanic/subjective nature of the dreamhunt experience. Na'vi spirituality isn't just empirical, after all, and has a deeply subjective, and entheogenic, experience, at its heart. It's the dreamhunt, after all, that allows for each Na'vi to undergo the necessary "second birth" in the process of becoming one of the people. Linking directly to the Tree of Souls isn't enough. It is the personal ordeal of the entheogenic experience of each individual, alone with his or her mind and his or her private experience of energy and visions, that makes one a true Na'vi.

It also implies that as sentient and self-aware beings, the Na'vi have a different relationship to their environment and themselves than the other beings they share their world with, just as is true for humans. It's not as simple as merely being an integrated part of the forest, such as is reflected in the simplistic claim that indigenous peoples are "one with their environment." The entheogen use implies that as ego-centered beings, we are consciously separated at a deep level – a level that can only be overcome by going within. No amount of external "tree hugging" will do the trick. Overcoming our sense of separation and lack of knowledge of the true self takes self-sacrifice and the willingness to privately endure the most challenging of tasks: facing ourselves in the most intimate recesses of our own minds and the expansion of our sense of awareness beyond the body and into our infinite natures.   True expanded awareness must be accomplished individually and privately. And to do that, it takes the right kinds of tools, be it worm and scorpion, or leaf and vine. When it comes to the deepest mysteries of the self, only the inward journey will suffice to bring true awareness and understanding. Only they can we be reborn into the "real" world of enhanced understanding.

All of this makes Jake's journey of becoming Toruk Makto all that much more complex and interesting. Here, we see that the first true intimation of Jake's relationship to Toruk was in the form of a psychedelic vision. His journey is primarily one of identity. In it, Jake must first expand his identity to include his avatar body. Then, in his quest to join the Na'vi, his identity begins to shift his cultural and racial allegiance, a choice for which Jake must eventually face serious consequences. Yet even here, his identity must shift again, for when he truly chooses the Na'vi and Eywa as his primary focus of identity, then he must face the challenge of Toruk. This challenge was first intimated to Jake during his dreamhunt when he saw himself riding the great beast. It was in his willing solo-journey into himself that this most crucial key was revealed. He would never fully be himself until he found his genuine connection to the larger energetic reality:

To be himself, to be reborn into himself, he had to embrace his greater nature as Toruk Makto and leader of the Na'vi people, fighting on behalf of Eywa, fighting on behalf of life.

It is true that in the end, Cameron presents the audience with a fairly simplistic moral tale, told in the style of a grand adventure. Eywa, despite protestations that she "doesn't take sides," clearly does, in the film, and humans are forcibly expelled from Pandora and "Eden" is restored through Jake's uncompromising willingness to be himself fully and completely, without regard to what consequences that might bring him. He was willing to sacrifice everything to live true to what he already knew about himself. It took more than love of a "woman" and a culture and an idyllic home to bring Jake to this, however. It also took his dreamhunt, his psychedelic exploration into his deepest awareness where he and he alone could face the truth of who he was. In the film, Jake becomes an extension of Eywa, acting selflessly on Eywa's and the people's behalf. So who is Jake? Is he the human? The avatar? Toruk Makto? Eywa? What is identity, and how does one know for sure, without clear introspection?

Beyond the easy and dualistic morality of the film lie deeper questions of the nature of the self, identity, and choice. And these are important questions for anyone, not just characters in a film, for aren't we all the main character in our own personal epic? What is your place, and how can you know that if you don't know who you are? Hug as many trees and shift your identity as much as you like, but are you willing to take the necessary journey within to find clarity?

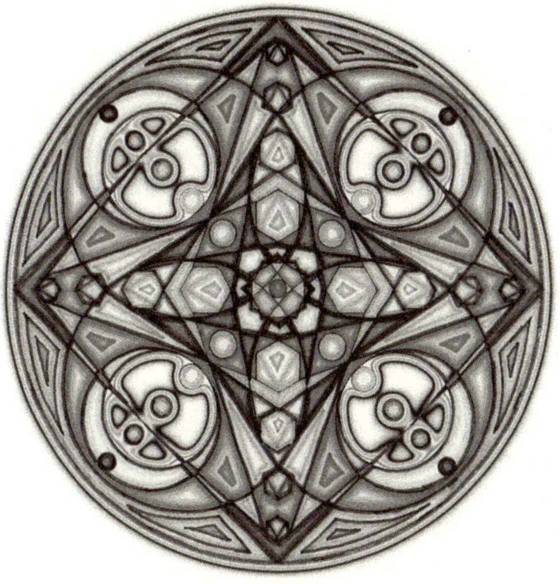

Visionary Art
Entheogens, and Communication with the Self

Introduction:

In the spring of 2010 I was asked to write about art and entheogens for an upcoming book, *Feminine Mysticism in Art: Artists Envisioning the Divine,* by Victoria Christian. What follows is my original write-up and reflects my initial thoughts on the subject. However, this didn't work for the book, so I ended up submitting an essay that focused on each artist individually, rather than examining recurring thematic elements as given here.

As this is not an art book, I do not have the specific images that are referenced in the essay. However, many of the pieces can be found on artists' websites:

www.danielmirante.com
www.martinahoffmann.com
www.galactivation.com
www.marieladelapaz.com
www.artofimagination.org/Pages/Cranmer

Given that I've analyzed this art according to the Entheological Paradigm, I thought that this essay would make a good fit for this book. However, I'd note that my analysis, as you might be able to guess, by now, is not necessarily what the artists themselves might say about their pieces and their significance. While my own focus does not emphasize the visionary nature of entheogens, for artists, this is a major reward for working with entheogens; the visionary inspiration they provide. Some of these artists most likely see the world in terms of spirits, realms, and mysterious encounters: all ideas that are ultimately discounted in my analysis. As with the other essays in this collection, what I'm interested in discussing here with this art is the fundamentals underneath it all – why it looks the way it does and why certain elements repeat across artists and time – in other words, the universal.

The Essay:

Art has been and always will be many things, but one fundamental truth of art is that it is primarily a process of communication with the self. What that "self" is remains to be defined, and will be explored in this essay. However, even at a cursory glance, one can see how art is a process of communication with the self simply by understanding how it is that art comes into existence. The artist works with his or her tools to give shape and form in two dimensions to something that does not exist in two dimensions. It is a translation of an image, replicated from without, conceived and experienced within, or discovered in the process of creation, into a representation that communicates *something*. That *something* can be intentional, accidental, archetypal, or indefinable. Yet it is there, and if it weren't for the journey taken by the artist into the self to produce it, it would not exist.

Art that is the product of visionary states of consciousness and the entheogenic journeys of the artist, such as much of the art of this section of the book, has a great deal to communicate and has played a fundamental role in the development of human cultures and consciousness. Historically, most visionary art has been produced within the confines of particular traditions and cultures, and therefore are reflective of cultural styles and concerns. The pieces shown here are all part of the contemporary quest for a new vision of reality and humanity's place within it. These images do not come from any specific tradition, but rather from the experiences and inspirations of the artists themselves. In order to understand the art, we need to understand the role of visionary states of consciousness and entheogenic experiences and how they translate into imagistic representations. A brief look at visionary art and human history will help us form an informed perspective on the art being presented here.

Visionary Art in Human History

Art, in multiple forms, and altered/visionary states of consciousness have always gone hand in hand. This is certainly true of the representational arts. Archeological evidence shows that the earliest paintings and carvings that humans produced in caves and secret grottos relate directly to altered states of consciousness, often through the ingestion of visionary plants and mushrooms. It is also clear that these representational art forms were expressive of early human societies' sense of "the sacred" or "the spiritual," however these terms may be understood. Representational art also marks the transition between pre-human and human consciousness, as it is a hallmark of culture, self-awareness, and a desire to communicate and express experiences and perceptions of the mysterious world in which humanity awoke to consciousness.

The creation of representational art has thus always coincided with humanity's journey into self-understanding, communication, and representation. It has been a means for humanity to represent itself and its world to itself in visible, communicative form. Yet even the earliest art forms transcend beyond the "ordinary" world into the strange and unusual forms of the "unseen," the "spiritual" and the "transcendent." Art, as a form of human expression, developed as a medium to communicate "the bigger picture," however that was conceived or experienced. It communicates beyond the immediately given into the complex realm of human experience and self-awareness.

The first artists were the shamans – those who bravely journeyed into the unknown realms of consciousness and awareness in order to experience and learn. Among the most powerful of the shaman's tools to experience altered states of consciousness have been the mind-altering plants and fungi. While knowledge of the ancient, and often, ongoing, use of psychedelic and entheogenic substances is becoming more common and widespread, many are still largely ignorant of the primary role these substances have had in human cultures, religions, and traditions throughout history, and their close connection to art.

The arc of human cultures and traditions can been viewed as quests for humans to understand their world and communicate that understanding to themselves. Among early humans, it was those who explored altered states of consciousness who were able to communicate and represent the most expanded view of what that world was and what humanity's role was within it. Knowledge of altered states of consciousness therefore became synonymous with knowledge of the sacred, or that which was more truly real than the appearances of "ordinary" reality. In order to gain more knowledge of these strange realms of experience and knowing, shamans made use of whatever tools were available to them. By far the most reliable, powerful, and consistent tools for opening up visionary states of consciousness were the entheogens: mind-altering plants, fungi, and substances that can profoundly affect human awareness and perception. Meditation, drumming, fasting, and other means were also used for entering into altered states, but evidence suggests that these were later derivations from the more direct route of entheogen ingestion.

Early art in Europe and Africa clearly show connections between art, spiritual representation, and entheogen use and visionary experience. Strangely elongated figures that blend human and animal characteristics with jagged lines of energy, geometric patterns with radial geometry and bilateral symmetry, sparkling figures, interwoven lines and grids: all clear representations of altered states of awareness and experience. Sometimes the connections to entheogens are obvious: depictions of mushroom eating shamans in ecstatic states of transformation, or mushroom effigies and spirit figures holding the divine plants in their hands.

Eventually, knowledge of the sacred plants and the visionary states of consciousness they made accessible became incorporated into what developed as cultural and religious traditions. Artistic representations of such forms of consciousness entered the imagistic vocabularies of cultures. Behind the art lay the experiences, but the art itself became a medium to communicate the experience or worldview for those who were not privy to the sacred trance or the ecstatic flight into the unknown. Art became a tool of communication of the scared experience and the unfolding of hidden orders of reality and human experience and often became stylized into particular cultural forms.

Whether or not entheogens and altered states of consciousness are made use of in religious and spiritual traditions today, we can still see the experiential origin of the art within the traditions that underlies the cultural grammar of images. The meditative and visionary techniques of the eastern traditions of Buddhism and Hinduism developed out of shamanic use of entheogenic mushrooms and plants, still in use in India and Nepal to this day among trantric practitioners. The radial symmetry of *mandalas* and *yantras* and the flowing, almost "psychedelic" imagery of *thankas* clearly reflect back on the visionary experiences of the trantric traditions.

In the west, the entheogenic origins of art and spirituality have been obfuscated and hidden; yet they still remain present for those who care to look. Mushrooms abound in Christian art, sometimes hidden, sometimes obvious. Representations of the Tree of Knowledge as mushrooms are common. The intricate creation of stained-glass windows as kaleidoscopic forms also harkens back to the visionary state produced by psychedelic substances.

Before the advent of Christianity, psychedelics played a key role in Greek culture, religion, and art. For 2,000 years, the Mystery Cults of Hellenic culture served up a psychedelic drink in the form of *kykeon*, most likely containing LSD. The realms that this drink opened up to initiates were expressed through Greek philosophy, art, mathematics, and geometry.

Further north, the tribal peoples of Europe used a variety of visionary plants and substances, only truly crushed as a cultural practice at the time of the Catholic Inquisition when "witches" were tortured and killed all across Europe. Amanita and psilocybe mushrooms, henbane, mandrake, datura, nightshade, opium, marijuana; all of these were used by European cultures, traces of which can be found in the geometric and interlaced artwork of the Celts and other northern European cultures.

Across the sea, in the Americas, entheogens, art, and visionary/spiritual experience went hand in hand perhaps even more than with the cultures already considered. In the American southwest and west coast, datura was the most commonly used entheogen. In southern California, ancient cave paintings depict the strange beings and geometric forms revealed by this dangerous plant. Throughout the Southwest and northern Mexico, cultures that were influenced by peyote developed intricate art forms of radial geometry and complex patterning, seen most vividly today in Huichol yarn paintings and weavings. Further south, mushroom (and other entheogens) using cultures such as the Maya and Aztec developed not only sophisticated styles of geometric art, but also writing systems, calendars, and complex mathematical systems. Entheogenic states of consciousness played (and continue to play) a highly significant role in the creation of beautifully colored textiles of complex patterns, grids, and various expressions of symmetry and interconnection found in Mayan cultures today.

Moving even further south, virtually all South American indigenous art and representational expression in the Amazon developed out of use of numerous variations of the ayahuasca drink. Higher up in the mountains, it was the hallucinogenic cacti that provided the right tools for opening up the vast realms of visionary consciousness that were then communicated through art and representational forms.

The contemporary art considered here follows in this ancient tradition of the shaman/artist exploring altered states of consciousness and then representing and exploring these experiences through the creation of art. As an explorer of altered states of consciousness myself, I am very interested in this process and what is generated from it. I believe that through an analysis of the art presented here, we can come to a naturalistic understanding of visionary art that both acknowledges and de-mystifies its sacred or spiritual nature. To do so, we will examine what this art represents, what it communicates, and how it is reflective of visionary and entheogenic states of consciousness and what that reveals about the nature of the self.

Entheogenic Experience

We can begin with a basic understanding of what entheogens are and what role they play in the human body. The word entheogen means, "generating the experience of god within," and was coined to replace the word "psychedelic," which was itself coined to replace the term "hallucinogen." Entheogen is meant to be reflective of the "sacred" quality of the experiences that these substances occasion and their use in ritual and ceremonial practice among traditional cultures and religions, as briefly reviewed above.

There are several families of entheogenic plants and fungi with the most significant for our conversation being the tryptamine family of entheogens. We will largely limit our discussion to this family as this is what is directly represented in the art that we are considering here and therefore is most revealing of the connections between entheogenic experience and artistic creation and communication.

Perhaps the most significant feature of the tryptamines is that they are endogenous to the human body, meaning that all humans naturally have tryptamines in their bodies at all times. Though their roles are still not fully understood scientifically, both Dimethyltryptamine (DMT, or N,N DMT) and 5 Methoxy Dimethyltryptamine (5-MeO-DMT) are found in all humans. These compounds are found in our lungs, blood, nervous system, and spinal fluid. Both compounds also function as neurotransmitters. Not only are they found in humans, but all mammal species as well. Given their ubiquitous presence, they have obviously played a role in mammalian evolution, and quite possibly a direct role in the evolution of human consciousness and self-awareness.

In the art that we are considering here, tryptamines were influential for several artists. The works by Ka, Mariela de la Paz, Martina Hoffman, and Scott Cranmer are all related to DMT in that they reference either ayahuasca or psilocybin mushrooms, and the works by Carey Thompson clearly suggest such connections. Ayahuasca is a DMT-containing brew made in the Amazon by indigenous cultures and is central to their traditions and lifeways. The DMT of the *Psychotria viridis* leaves is accessed through combining them with the monoamineoxidase inhibitor of the *Banisteriopsis caapi* vine and boiling them down together into a thick and pungent brew. DMT is also the base molecule for the psilocin and psilocybin found in psychedelic mushrooms.

When consumed in any form, DMT is a powerful chemical catalyst. Though it is already present in the human body, when consumed in relatively very small amounts, in the range of 20 – 100 mg, it can radically change how one sees and understands the nature of the self and the world. Many in the contemporary Western world enjoy smoking DMT for a very fast, very powerful experience that begins almost instantaneously and comes to a conclusion within less than 10 minutes. In more traditional settings, with the ingestions of ayahuasca or mushrooms, the DMT can take up to an hour to really come into effect and then will last for several more hours, with mushrooms generally lasting somewhat longer than ayahuasca, despite the fact that ayahuasca tends to produce a more powerful experience. Smoked DMT, however, can be far more powerful experientially than either ayahuasca or mushrooms. Smoked 5-MeO-DMT is the most powerful and radical of all.

DMT experiences are extremely visual in nature, especially when eyes are closed. At times, the visual experience behind closed eyes is completely unique and has no relationship to what is seen with eyes open, and one can toggle between two completely distinct sets of visual impressions merely by alternately opening and closing the eyes. At other times, an immersive visionary scene might be identical regardless of whether one has open or closed eyes. And at other times, even when things appear "normal" with open eyes, or relatively so, vast and complex images can appear behind closed eyes.

Actual visionary content can vary tremendously from person to person and from experience to experience. However, there are some universal features of DMT experiences, regardless of culture, tradition, or context, that reveal significant underlying features. At the most basic level, entheogenic experiences are experiences of energy. Such experiences are palpable within the body, visible to open and closed eyes, and synesthetic in nature. When one ingests an entheogen, one's ability to perceive and experience energy is greatly enhanced and amplified. Visually, the effect is quite dramatic.

Complex patterning, interrelated forms, intersecting geometries, color spectrums and gradients, fractal repetitions, and crystalline formations are all manifestations of the mathematical quality of energy. Energy is always expressed in precise mathematical formations – all energy is, in some form or another, quantifiable (even if we don't know how to measure it precisely). This is true from the sub-atomic particles of quantum physics that exhibit intricate bilateral symmetry to the wave forms of electromagnetic energy produced by the heart and brain to the currents of energy that sweep across the vast cosmic stretches of the universe and reach our awareness through our telescopes and scientific instruments. Everything that can be experienced or known in reality is energy in one form or another. The underlying foundation of the visionary experiences occasioned by DMT are experiences of perceiving energy. This energy can be both seen and felt in the DMT state. At the most basic level, consumption of DMT can be said to enhance an individual's ability to perceive and experience certain forms of energy and this is clearly reflected in the universal perceptions of geometry, patterns, gradients, and fractal and symmetrical forms.

Entheogenic Geometry and Symmetry

A number of the pieces in this collection have clear visual references to the geometric and patterned structure of the DMT/entheogenic experience. Take "Eye Wish," by Ka, for example. Geometric forms underlie the more representational visionary content of the image. Often referred to as "sacred" geometry, we could instead identify such structures as foundational geometry. These geometric structures are readily found within nature, as well as within the entheogenic, visionary state. All of existence is found to have underlying geometry. Everything that can be observed and experienced within nature shares in this universal feature and the visionary state is no exception. Geometric structures are mathematical in nature, and therefore provide structure to permutations of energy, which is itself mathematical in nature.

We can see a similar emphasis on underlying geometric form in "Singularity," by Carey Thompson, and "Eagle Shakti," by Daniel Mirante. In these, as well as "Mothership," by Scott Cranmer, "Priestess Mariela," and "Ayahuasca Mama," by Mariela de la Paz, "Caught in the Web," and "Firekeeper," by Martina Hoffman, we also see an emphasis on mirrored, bilateral symmetry.

This form of symmetry is highly significant for the entheogenic visionary state and manifests across several different levels of experience. Let's deal with the visual level first. The energy and images that one can perceive and experience in entheogenic states of consciousness are incredibly varied and no two experiences are precisely alike. Especially with closed eyes, all manner of imagery may appear to the visionary. When visions are especially intense, visionaries can feel as though they are completely immersed in another reality or exist in a disembodied state in a sea of pure conscious energy. Traditionally, in shamanic and visionary cultures, these visionary states of consciousness are understood as being in some sense real and existing outside of the imagination of the visionary. I do not think that such an explanation is necessary, however, as the entheogenic experience is more easily understood as a highly sophisticated interactive mirror of the self.

The experiences that occur in an entheogenic state are always a reflection of the one who is undergoing the experience. Given the understanding that entheogens open one up to the perception and experience of ones own energy, all that is revealed in the visionary state is a reflection of ones energy. Visually, when one is centered, relaxed, and open, the energy perceived in the entheogenic state tends to exhibit extraordinarily high degrees of symmetry, either radial, or mirrored, bilateral symmetry. When in radial form, energy often appears kaleidoscopic or mandala-like. We can see many radial forms and structures in the art pieces being considered here.

Human Geometry

However, the experience of energy, especially when ones attention is grounded in awareness of the body, can very often take on mirrored bilateral symmetry. When one considers the human body as an energetic system, it is clear to see that we are geometric/fractal forms with distinct bilateral symmetry. In fact, we can also see that life forms in general are divided by their overall geometry and symmetry. Early life forms were of radial geometry – one only need consider a single-celled organism to see that this is true. Plants and forms of sea life developed branch fractal geometry combined with radial geometry and alternating symmetry.

"Higher" life forms are built on a different geometry, however, and this geometry involves infinity loops. Like the interwoven trees in Daniel Mirante's "Deep Ecology Web," the bilateral symmetry of vertebrates is based on infinity loop-generated anatomy. Human anatomy, as with other vertebrates, is constructed through a central column of infinity loops. At our heads, we have the infinity loop of the lobes of the brain, the seat of consciousness, which energetically manifests in our bodies from its infinite source. Our sense organs of eyes, ears and nostrils are also manifestations of this same infinity loop of energy. From this infinite source of energy, the fractal branch patterns of our nervous system stretch out through our bodies, allowing us to have physical experience and sensation through touch and bodily awareness.

At our heart, the infinite source of the energy of love, the primary energy of existence, shapes into the two sets of chambers of our heart and the lungs, where we also find DMT. From this interconnected set of infinity loops, life-giving blood nourishes our body as the electrical pulse of our heart sends out electromagnetic waves through the fractal branch pattern of our vascular system.

Lastly, the infinite source of the energy of creation is located in our reproductive system where the infinity loop is mirrored into the sides of the sex organs and the testes and ovaries. When these manifestations of infinite energy come together, new life takes shape through the ongoing fractal expression of the evolution of all life through reproduction.

Thus, when a human looks into a mirror, literally, one sees a being that has certain geometric features: bilateral mirrored symmetry with a centralized core built of infinity loops and fractal branch geometry. Within the physical proportions of our body also is found the "golden mean," the primary ratio of what is considered "sacred" geometry.

These are the same geometric and energetic structures that one can also observe and experience in the entheogenic state, especially at high levels of tryptamine consumption. The visions produced by entheogens literally are a mirror of the self – just in a different form of perception. Artistic creations that represent this form of visionary experience therefore are clearly a communication with the self. It is a representation of the artist's experience and inspiration, represented in two-dimensional form, that communicates something of the "sacred" experience to the viewer. It communicates that "seeing this way is possible" within the context of the actual image. It calls the viewer to see the image as the self.

Body Posture as Energy

The physical postures of figures presented in these images are highly significant, as well, and are immediately related to the entheogenic experience and the nature of the self that is revealed within it. In Mariela's works, "Priestess," and "Ayahuasca Mama," we see the geometric form of the physically and energetically open woman – arms symmetrical, hands open and turned up, legs open and knees bent, exposing the open power of the vulva. In "Priestess," Mariela shows us a stance of power, symmetrical, open, firmly grounded. In "Ayahuasca Mama," she shows us a woman who is surrendered and open, her bilateral symmetry of her physical form resting in the opening flower of radial geometry that unfolds beneath and within her, bordered by the masculine power of the erect cacti.

Stances and postures such as these are common in entheogenic experiences. When the visionary relaxes deeply into the experience of energy, body postures and movements that exhibit mirrored bilateral symmetry are common. This is especially true with high-level experiences of DMT and 5-MeO-DMT. In these states, individuals surrender fully and relax into their energy, having abandoned the limiting confines of the ego and the energetic constructs of the mind. When this occurs, their energy naturally flows into a centered, mirrored state. Arms and hands move in unison with each other, mirroring each other in fluid, natural movement. Legs mirror each other as well and the entire body flows together as a unified energetic system with waves of energy undulating up and down the spine. In particularly powerful experiences, the ultra-fine vibrations of this energy can be felt throughout ones entire being. The key for the visionary is to relax fully into the energy and surrender to it.

We also see images of individuals centered in their energy with mirrored bilateral symmetry in "Eagle Shakti," "Mothership," "Singularity," and in Martina Hoffman's pieces. Many of these images show open, mirrored hands, reflective of an open energetic posture. Within the overwhelming energetic torrent of the entheogenic experience, it is precisely this open posture that allows the visionary to surrender most fully to the experience.

Of these, "Caught in the Web," shows the most open, surrendered posture. Typical of the ayahuasca experience, the woman at the bottom of the image is shown fully surrendered to the purging power of the medicine. Her arms lie at her side, palms up and hands open, as the medicine removes her energetic blocks through the action of purging. Resisting such energy can be horrendous for the visionary. The only real option is to surrender and let the purge take place, for only then will ones energy more into a more relaxed and healing state.

In contrast, in "Firekeeper," we see a more protective energetic stance. Mirrored bilateral symmetry is still apparent, however. Here the figure protects the sanctity of her womb space, yet stands confidently in the infinite power of her consciousness, which emanates from her head in curving patterns of energy.

Images of Unity and Balance

Many of these images also show how specific visionary images can arise from the perception of mirrored bilateral symmetry. In "Singularity," we see complex figures with bilateral symmetry, combining multiple layers of symbolic imagery of cultural and natural origin. In "Mothership," we see the intertwined image of a feminine figure with interlacing symmetrical rainbows, joining into a fractal-like regression of repeating patterns forming a mushroom with distinct eye-like features.

It is no accident that images that arise in the visionary state are reflective of the energy of the viewer. The visionary experience is a mirror experience within the Divine Imagination. Within this energetic state of perception, the individual is opened up to the infinite nature of the mind and of energy. Here communication with the self takes place in varied forms. The self is both that which is perceiving and that which is perceived. How one chooses to react to what is seen and how one chooses to think about it influences how the vision unfolds in a sophisticated feedback loop. Underneath it all is the pure energy of being: mathematical, balanced, symmetrical, unitary.

What virtually all of these images show is the unitary and interconnected nature of all manifestations of energy. The images by Mariela de la Paz that do not exhibit symmetry are still filled with representations of the energetic patterning of reality. They present a way of seeing the world: the way of seeing that is made available by entheogenic perception and experience. "Caught in the Web," "Singularity," and "Eye

Wish" all show the fundamental connection of all things and the interrelated nature of our experience of reality.

What the entheogenic experience reveals is that all things are united in their energetic natures. There is nothing that exists that is not energy in some form, and there is no real boundary to energy, for it is a continuum of interrelated spectrums. Within the infinite energy continuum of reality, there is the experience of the self, the experience of being. What unites all spectrums and manifestations of energy is the unitary experience of "I am." This is a knowledge that can never be destroyed, for it is the very ground of experience. Within the entheogenic experience, the knowledge that "I am" persists, even if the nature of that self is not understood by the rational or egoic mind.

Reflections of the Self

The art here shows this expanded view of the self. It is presented imagistically, sometimes as a scene, sometimes as a mirror image of the self as directly experienced in the entheogenic state. In imagistic form, we are reminded that we are that sacred geometry, we are that energy, we are that connection between all things, and we are that experience of "I am." The art is calling us to awaken to who and what we truly are: energetic embodiments of the "I am." The conclusion is clear: we are the Divine Being. All of reality is contained within us, within our experience of "I am." We are the sacred.

The canvas can only contain what the artist chooses to place upon it. Through the process of creation, the artist interacts with him or herself and the canvass as the surface of a projection. Just like in the entheogenic state, all that is revealed upon that canvas comes from the self. What is revealed both in this art and in the entheogenic state is the communication that we are more than what we think we are. We are human, but what does it mean to be human? What does it mean to live with the responsibility of who and what we are? If all of reality is contained within us and mirrored in our experience, then we are the ones who are responsible for the world we find ourselves in. We are the ones who are responsible for recognizing the true connections between all things and the unitary nature of reality.

This art speaks to the fundamental human truth of where we find ourselves in our evolution and development here on planet Earth: the time has come to recognize the truth of ourselves and take responsibility for it. How we choose to live with each other, other beings, and this earth is our choice. Will we choose to recognize the patterns that connect us to all things and live in balance, symmetry, and harmony with it, or choose otherwise? Will we live in balance and symmetry with all the aspects of ourselves, or will we foolishly indulge in asymmetry and imbalance? The choice is ours. Always and forever. This art calls to us: Choose wisely, for it is you.

My Birthday Wish – 11/26/2010

My wish on my birthday is this: for all individuals to courageously accept the reality of what is now occurring – The Genuine Awakening of the Consciousness of the One.

The Time has Come.

It is time for humanity to let go of all our illusions, projections, fantasies, fears, attachments, beliefs, and all the rest that limits us from the direct and immediate experience of who and what we truly are: The Infinite in Human Form.

I wish for all individuals to freely and consciously participate in this process, for the wave is already moving, and all can either ride with it, or be left in its wake.

I wish for everyone to let go of all those things that they believe that limit, confine, and constipate them in their being and energy. Let go of your Religions! Let go of your Spiritualities! Let go of your pet theories of Reality! Let go of all the Bull Shit and Let It Pass! Let go of your Machine Elves, your Angles, your Buddhas, your Past Lives, your Karma, your Avatars, your Ascended Masters, your Saviors, your Spirit Guides, your Gurus, your Lamas, your Shamans, your Holy Books, your Sacred Scriptures, your Prophesies, your 2012, your Sacred Calendars!

Take every idol of your home, heart, body and mind and burn it in the Infinite Fire of the One Universal Energetic Reality that You Are! Let go of everything you've ever thought and ever believed and expand into your Full Infinite Energetic Nature.

Know that You are The ONE! It is your choice! Every individual is free to choose, and every individual is responsible for him or herself.

So take responsibility and BE WHO YOU ARE! Take courage! Fill your lungs with air, look into your heart, and Burn All Illusions in the Infinite Fire of Universal Love!

Let go of your judgment, your victim-hood, your righteousness, your faith, your fear, your blame, your envy, your manipulations, your drama, and all that you use to make excuses for yourself. There is no one to blame, for you are ALL!

Be the Infinite Love of the Self that you TRULY ARE.

Love universally, and you will be FREE.

In freedom, may all be reborn in to the True Infinite Reality that We Are!

Right here. Right now. This Very Moment!

With Infinite, Universal, Unconditional, Uncompromising, Fearless, Fierce, Ruthless and Relentless LOVE!

- Your Self

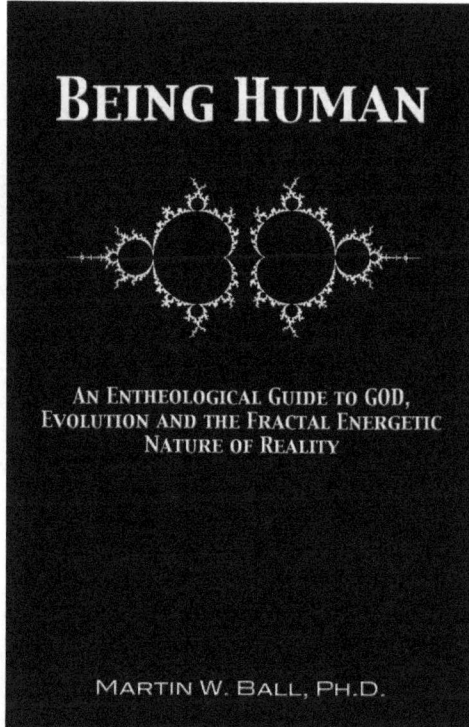

New by Martin W. Ball, Ph.D.

Tell it to the Mystic Toad: *What Participants at Burning Man Confessed at the God Box Theme Camp*

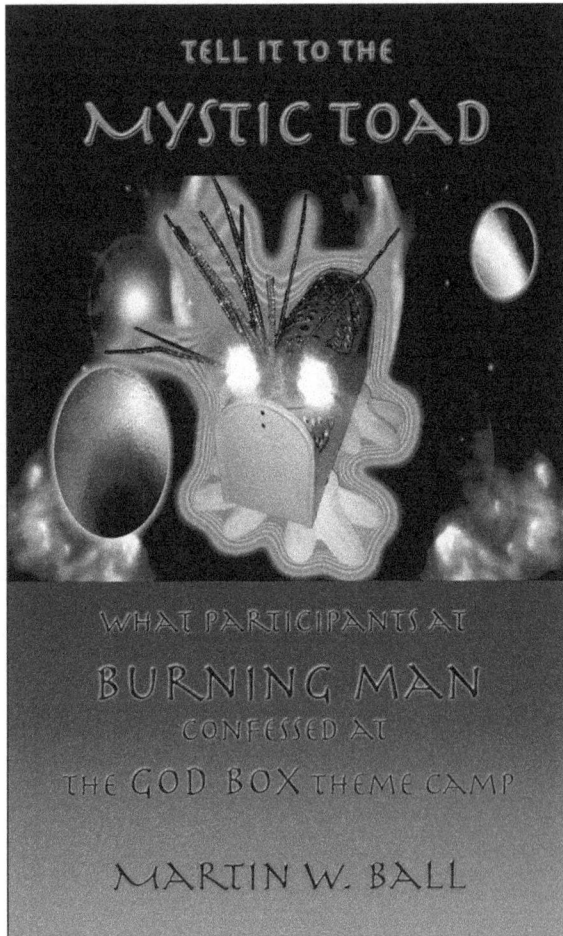

If given the chance, what would Burners confess before coming face to face with God?
In this new book, readers are treated to glimpses into the minds of revelers at Burning Man as they shared their inner thoughts in the Book of Confessions. Humorous, absurd, and poignant, these brief revelations showcase both the uniqueness and universality of the human heart.

Original music by Martin Ball is available at iTunes

New Album, 2011: *Kaleidoscopic*

Additional albums available on iTunes:

The Medicine Show
Songs of the Mystic Fire
Music for the Entheogenic Evolution
Infinite Horizons
Music of Aurduin

Martin's music is an ever-shifting mix of instrumentation, genres, and styles, blending elements of world, electronica, reggae, alternative, Asian, Middle Eastern, Native American, and South American sounds into an intoxicating and inspiring mix. Each album is a new exploration into previously uncharted territory, opening the mind, liberating the heart, and moving the body.

For more information on the work of Martin W. Ball, Ph.D. and the Entheological Paradigm, visit the following websites:

Martin's personal website:
www.martinball.net

The Official Entheological Paradigm website:
www.entheological-paradigm.net

The Entheogenic Evolution Podcast:
www.entheogenic.podomatic.com

The Entheological Paradigm on YouTube:
www.youtube.com/EntheogenicEvolution

PDF writings and ebooks:
www.scribd.com/Martin Ball